What Is Christianity?

What Is Christianity?

Douglas Jacobsen

Registered Office(s)
John Wiley & Sons, Inc., 111 River Street, Hoboken, NJ 07030, USA
John Wiley & Sons Ltd, The Atrium, Southern Gate, Chichester, West Sussex, PO19 8SQ, UK

Editorial Office
9600 Garsington Road, Oxford, OX4 2DQ, UK

For details of our global editorial offices, customer services, and more information about Wiley products visit us at www.wiley.com.

Wiley also publishes its books in a variety of electronic formats and by print-on-demand. Some content that appears in standard print versions of this book may not be available in other formats.

Library of Congress Cataloging-in-Publication Data
Names: Jacobsen, Douglas G. (Douglas Gordon), 1951- author.
Title: What is Christianity? : a short introduction to Christianity and its
    major sub-traditions / Douglas Jacobsen.
Description: Hoboken, NJ : John Wiley & Sons, 2022. | Includes
    bibliographical references and index.
Identifiers: LCCN 2021024449 (print) | LCCN 2021024450 (ebook) | ISBN
    9781119746690 (paperback) | ISBN 9781119746706 (pdf) | ISBN
    9781119746713 (epub)
Subjects: LCSH: Christian sects. | Christianity. | Church history.
Classification: LCC BR157 .J33 2022 (print) | LCC BR157 (ebook) | DDC
    280–dc23
LC record available at https://lccn.loc.gov/2021024449
LC ebook record available at https://lccn.loc.gov/2021024450

Cover image: © Kevin Carden/123rf
Cover design by Wiley

Set in 9.5/12.5 pt and STIXTwoText by Integra Software Services, Pondicherry, India

SKYE6EE48D7-BBB8-4BDB-B224-A83829DB4F65_102721

For Hudson

Contents

List of Figures

List of Tables

Introduction

What Is Christianity?

Christianity is the most popular and influential religion in human history. Launched by Jesus of Nazareth two thousand years ago, the Christian movement currently has more than two and a half billion members. Christians are now located in every country on earth, and they represent the majority of the population in Europe, Latin America, North America, Oceania, and southern Africa. But what exactly constitutes Christianity? What does this religion stand for? What makes Christianity Christian? Why have so many people embraced it?

More than one hundred years ago, a professor at a prestigious German university decided to provide answers to all these questions. He arrived at the university lecture hall a few minutes before six o'clock in the morning when it was still dark outside, and the walk across campus had invigorated him. When he stepped up to the podium, not a seat in the house was empty. Six hundred students (all of them male because women would not be admitted to the university until 1908) and a smattering of faculty colleagues had their eyes fixed on him as he began the day's address. "What is Christianity?" he asked, and they were counting on him to supply an answer. The year was 1900. The place was the University of Berlin. The speaker was Adolph von Harnack, one of the most brilliant and well-known scholars in the world.

Professor Harnack did not disappoint. He gave them a simple and straightforward answer because, he told them, the gospel itself is simple. Christianity at its purest and best is the religion of Jesus, the message that Jesus himself proclaimed. It focuses on three things: the fatherhood of God, the infinite value of the human soul, and the commandment to love everyone. In a nutshell, that was it. That is the essence of Christianity. Christians had advocated many other beliefs and practices during the movement's long history, but, according to Harnack, those other things were largely superfluous. The only thing that really matters is Jesus's core teaching. This is the gospel – the message Christianity has to share with the world – and that gospel (or "good news") is simple.

Something even more basic was at stake, however. For Harnack, the simple gospel of Jesus is not merely the essence of Christianity, it is the quintessence of religion itself. A humanistic scholar who affirmed the validity of science, Harnack served as the first president of the Kaiser Wilhelm society which later became the Max Planck Society for the Advancement of Science, one of the most prestigious centers for the study of human evolution in the world. Harnack was interested in human origins, and he believed that it is religion – the spiritual impulse that leads people to wonder about the mystery of life and how they are called to live – that makes *Homo sapiens* into something more than merely smart animals. For Harnack, a proper understanding of the gospel of Jesus was not merely the key to understanding Christianity, it was the key for understanding what makes any of us human. And that is why 600 students voluntarily crowded into a university lecture hall at six o'clock in the morning for fifteen weeks in a row: to hear someone explain who they were called to be as followers of Jesus *and* who they were as human beings.

The German state church was not impressed with Harnack's views or erudition. Traditional German Christians thought his interpretation downplayed Christianity's traditional emphasis on personal salvation and correct doctrine, and they initially tried to block his promotion to the University of Berlin when it was announced in 1888. Ultimately Kaiser Wilhelm II was forced to intervene personally to make sure Harnack got the job. Despite the church's worries, Harnack himself was deeply committed to Christianity, and his lectures were crafted to provide university students with a positive view of Christianity that was fully compatible with modern learning. He hoped that university students would be so inspired by the message of Jesus that they would leave the university intent on making the German nation a place where "justice is done, no longer by the aid of force, but by free obedience to the good...not by legal regulations but by the ministry of love."[1] He wanted his students, and everyone else who heard or read his lectures, to become better Jesus-following Christians and more intelligent, caring citizens. That is how he envisioned Christianity: as the highest expression of religion itself, a faith focused on goodness and love, and the solution to all of humanity's problems.

Except it wasn't. Just a few years after delivering his lectures, Harnack's own actions undercut his claims. During the early months of World War I, he was one of ninety-three German intellectuals who composed a document entitled "To the Civilized World," which justified atrocities committed by the German army during its infamous Rape of Belgium. In this statement he and his professorial peers argued that anyone "inciting Mongolians [i.e., Asians] and negroes against the white race, ha[d] no right whatsoever to call themselves upholders of civilization."[2] Harnack may have thought Christianity was the best and most perfect religion for all people, times, and places, but it did not prevent him from rationalizing wanton violence against civilians and championing the cause of German racial supremacy.

Christianity has not been a wellspring of universal goodness for humankind. Christians have contributed much that is good to the world, but they have also done significant harm. They have believed Jesus's message of love for all people, but have often failed to act in loving, or even decent, ways. And Christianity cannot serve as the sole arbiter of human religiosity. Different religions provide humankind with different visions of the world as it is and could be, they offer different pathways to and definitions of salvation, and they advocate different ideals and values. Christianity is a powerful and inspiring religion, but it is not the simple religion that Harnack described.

In contrast to Harnack's idealistic portrayal, this book offers a more empirical examination of what Christians have believed, how they have acted, how they have organized themselves, how they have spread their message around the world, and what challenges they are facing today. There is no intention to either criticize or praise the movement; the only goal is fair and accurate description. That said, this book is more than a mere recital of facts and numbers quantifying Christianity from the outside. It also looks at Christianity from the inside, trying to explain Christianity's spiritual appeal and why so many people around the globe have embraced it.

One obvious fact about Christianity is that it is a far different movement today than it was a century ago when Harnack gave his university lectures. In 1900, two-thirds of the world's Christians still lived in Europe. Today, only a quarter of the world's Christians reside in Europe and about 10 percent live in North America. The rest, two-thirds of all the Christians in the world, live in the Global South (Africa, Asia, and Latin America). The internal composition of Christianity has also been transformed. In 1900, three major Christian traditions (Eastern Orthodoxy, Roman Catholicism, and Protestantism) dominated the Christian movement. Now there are four major traditions. The addition is Pentecostalism, and this new tradition, which currently attracts one out of every five Christians globally, has dramatically altered the Christian landscape.[3] Simultaneously, the terrain of global politics has been fundamentally reordered. In 1900, half the world's people were ruled by European colonial governments. Today those former colonies are independent nations, and the Christians who live in them are fully independent of Western Christian control. Christianity is no longer a European religion with a periphery everywhere else; Christianity has become a postcolonial, global faith with many different centers.

This book describes Christianity in eight chapters. Chapter 1 explains how the movement got started, and how within 500 years a small group of followers of Jesus grew into a religion that had a membership that spread across a massive region of the world, ranging from Ireland in the northwest to the southern tip of the Indian subcontinent. Chapter 1 also traces how Christianity changed from a loosely structured and fluid movement into a religion comprised of separately organized and distinct Christian traditions. Today, Christianity is housed in four major traditions – Eastern Orthodoxy, Catholicism, Protestantism, and Pentecostalism – and these four traditions account for about 97 percent of all the Christians in the world. Chapters 2 through 5 explain each of these traditions in turn.

The remainder of the book deals with the characteristics of Christianity as a whole. Chapter 6 describes Christianity's recent expansion around the world and the changing attitudes of Christians in both the Global North (Europe and North America) and the Global South (Africa, Asia, Latin America, and Oceania). Chapter 7 describes the dramatically different experiences of Christians around the world today. Some Christians are persecuted; others are persecutors. Some Christians are wealthy; many are poor. In some regions Christianity is growing; elsewhere it is in decline. Despite all of these differences, most Christians continue to see themselves as members of one religion. Chapter 8 explores this sense of Christian connectedness, describing what most Christians hold in common while also reflecting on a variety of religious challenges that Christianity is currently facing as a global movement. The Conclusion returns to the main question of the book and argues that Christianity today is what it has been throughout its long history: a religion that is still in the process of forming and reforming itself in response to changing circumstances and in light of its memory of Jesus.

Notes

1 Adolph Harnack, *What Is Christianity?* translated by Thomas Bailey Saunders (New York: Harper and Row, 1957), p. 112. Harnack's lectures were originally published in German in 1900 under the title *Das Wesen des Christentums*, which could literally be translated as "The Essence of Christianity." They were published in English in 1902 using the present title.

2 Professors of Germany, "To the Civilized World," *The North American Review* 210:756 (August 1919), pp. 284–287, https://www.jstor.org/stable/pdf/25122278. pdf?acceptTC=true (accessed September 8, 2020).

3 The demographic information included in this book represents the author's best estimates based on a variety of sources. The most complete and reliable source of information is the World Christian Database (https://www.worldchristiandatabase. org) and it has been consulted frequently. The numbers used here are not, however, taken directly from the WCD. They have sometimes been adjusted based on other information (from, for example, the United Nations or different national census figures) and the reporting categories differ from those of the WCD. Numbers in this book have been consistently rounded off to reflect that they are indeed estimates and not actual headcounts of Christians in different traditions, nations, or regions of the world. The goal has been to include all people who self-identify as Christian wherever they may live and whatever they may believe.

1

Christian Beginnings

The religion called Christianity did not spring into existence with its identity already fully developed and finalized. At first, Christians did not even know what to call themselves. The New Testament book of Acts refers to them simply as "followers of the Way" and infers that the term "Christians" was first used by others, possibly as a derogatory means of distinguishing disciples of Christ from other kinds of Jews. What seems clear is that Jesus had a powerful impact on his closest friends and associates and that those allies were able to communicate their enthusiasm about Jesus to others. In a sense, Christianity began as something like a fan club for Jesus. This is not meant as criticism, but merely as description. A fan club is held together by its devotion to a person, not by the ideas or ideals that demarcate its identity. Earliest Christianity was indeed something like a fan club: it was a movement of devotion to Jesus long before it developed a clear and distinct sense of its own religious identity.

Religious identity is a group phenomenon. Everyone has their own spiritual sense of who they are, but religions are bigger than any one individual. A religion is a community that a person joins, or is born into, that connects participants with the divine (or more generally with "the transcendent") and provides guidance for the journey of life. Religions are not meant to be easily modified to conform to one's wishes; indeed, few people want their religion to be pliable and undemanding. Religions are instead expected to provide a standard to which individuals conform, an ideal worthy of utmost human effort. People change their lives to fit their religion, not the other way around.

Religious identity consists of the beliefs, actions, values, personality traits, affectivities, and organizational structures that a religious community champions and shares with others. This does not mean that every member of the group agrees about everything. No group of people is ever that uniform. What it does mean is that members of the group hold enough things more-or-less in common that they feel a sense of belonging together. They recognize each other as family. They understand how people in the group think and know how members of the group feel about themselves, about others, and about the things they hold sacred.

What Is Christianity? First Edition. Douglas Jacobsen.
© 2022 John Wiley & Sons Ltd. Published 2022 by John Wiley & Sons Ltd.

When Christianity first began, it had not yet figured out its own religious identity. Christians weren't fully sure what they believed or didn't believe as a group, and there were no fixed rules about who belonged or didn't belong. There was as yet neither a New Testament nor a church hierarchy to supply answers. They had the Hebrew scriptures, but they were not quite sure how to interpret them; for that matter, they were not sure if Christianity was a new kind of Judaism or something else. As a group, Christians simply had not spent enough time together to develop a corporate personality, and they had no idea how to institutionally organize themselves or even if institutionalizing the movement was a proper goal. They all loved Jesus, but Christianity was not yet a religion. It was still just a loosely connected social movement of people on "the way."

It would be wrong to see these early Christians as totally adrift. That is clearly not accurate. Everyone agreed that Jesus was their guide and teacher, and they were all quite certain that a new age of divine blessing was dawning, but the movement was surprisingly open-ended. Lots of rules, regulations, and practices would be implemented later, and once they were in place Christians often treated them as if they had always been essential elements of the movement, but most had not. When Christianity began, it was a movement in search mode. Christians possessed a handful of ideas and inclinations that they were spiritually willing to bet their lives on, but they had not yet deciphered what it all meant. Figuring that out would literally take centuries, and there would always be multiple answers rather than just one. Instead of ending up with just one uniform and ubiquitous Christian identity, Christianity ended up with a number of different but overlapping and interrelated identities. These varied packages of Christian beliefs and practices are called traditions, and this chapter recounts how the original fledgling Christian movement slowly evolved over five or six hundred years to become an organized religion housed in multiple different traditions.

The Jewish Roots of Christianity

Jesus was a Jew, and Judaism is the source of many of the ideas and commitments that still characterize Christianity today. While the precise origins of Judaism are largely lost in the mists of history, the Hebrew scriptures assert that the Jewish people were called into existence by God and given a special role in the human story. The Hebrew scriptures include a vivid account of exodus from Egypt and conquest of Palestine, but the archaeological records from this time period (thirteenth century BCE) reflect a much slower and less dramatic progression of events that eventually gave birth to Israel and to Jewish religious consciousness. Whatever the process, it seems clear that by about 1000 BCE an Israelite kingdom had been established in Palestine, with its religious life focused on rituals performed at the Temple in Jerusalem.

In 587 BCE, Palestine was conquered by the powerful Babylonian emperor Nebuchadnezzar II. Many Jews were exiled to Persia (now Iraq and Iran), and the Jerusalem Temple was destroyed. Without a temple, Jews developed other mechanisms for preserving their faith, most notably the *synagogue*, a place where Jews could gather to pray and to discuss religious and moral matters. Jews started returning to Palestine around 540 BCE and promptly rebuilt the Jerusalem Temple, but synagogues remained in use as local meeting places for Jews wherever they lived. Several different dynasties conquered and ruled post-exile Palestine, but in the 140s BCE a Jewish state was reestablished in the region. That kingdom was of relatively short duration; it was subsumed into the Roman Empire in 63 BCE. From that juncture until 1948, Jews had no land they could call their own.

By the time of the Roman occupation, assorted groups of Jews had developed their own different ways of making sense of God, themselves, and their historical experience. Prominent Jewish sub-groups included the Pharisees, who stressed the law and personal piety; the Sadducees, who emphasized traditional temple worship; the Zealots, who were violently opposed to Roman rule; and the Qumran community that assumed the end of the world was near and that a final battle between good and evil was about to commence. The Samaritans, another quasi-Jewish group, claimed descent from two of Israel's ancient tribes, Ephraim and Manasseh. In addition, an increasing number of Gentiles (non-Jews) were calling themselves God-fearers and adopting many of Judaism's ideas and values without formally becoming Jews themselves.

This was the complex world of Jewish faith into which Jesus was born and which shaped the early Christian movement. Christianity retained many of the basic ideas and practices of Judaism. The synagogue morphed into the church, and the diversity of perspectives within Judaism prepared the way for the diversity of beliefs and practices that soon came to characterize the early Christian community. Imbedded in the matrix of first-century Judaism, Christianity emerged as a new and distinct religious movement led by a backcountry prophet named Jesus of Nazareth.

Jesus and the Gospel

Jesus was an unlikely leader. Neither a priest nor a scholar, Jesus lived his first thirty years in relative obscurity as the son of Mary and her husband Joseph, a carpenter in the small town of Nazareth in the region known as Galilee. Then, for just a few years before he was killed, he took on the role of a wandering Jewish prophet and teacher, at first in the rural region where he had been raised and later for a very short time in Jerusalem.

His message was simple but profound. Jesus affirmed much of the Judaism of his day, including the Golden Rule (which Jews usually expressed in the negative as "do not do to others what you would not want done to you"), but Jesus frequently added his own twist to these teachings. Some of his additions – the folksy way he referred to God as "abba" (best translated as "daddy"), his willingness to bend the law to accommodate human frailty, his claim that he was able to forgive sins – were troubling to traditional Jews, and some Jewish leaders plainly disliked Jesus and his movement.

His message was also troubling to Rome. Jesus spoke of a coming "kingdom of God" and described his own actions as the dawning of that kingdom. He instructed his followers to give appropriate respect to Caesar (the Roman Emperor), but he also told them to give their complete obedience to God, a qualification that obviously limited any loyalty owed to Caesar. And, while he did not seek political power for himself, he refused to cower when Rome's political appointees detained and interrogated him. His behavior seemed potentially subversive to an empire that demanded absolute obedience, and Rome responded vigorously. Using the gruesome spectacle of execution on a cross, the Empire eliminated Jesus and sent a public message to his followers that insolence in the face of imperial authority would not be tolerated.

Jerusalem's residents, and many of Jesus's own closest followers, thought that was the end of the matter. His male disciples were despondent and ready to abandon the cause. But some of his female friends began to claim they had seen Jesus alive, and soon his male disciples were making the same claim. They believed that somehow Jesus had been resurrected from the dead and had been given a new and glorious body. They also came to believe that this resurrected Jesus had given them a task to accomplish: they were to continue the work that Jesus had started, preaching the gospel message throughout the world, to every person, in every nation, in every tongue, and they were not to stop until they reached the ends of the earth.

The fourth-century historian Eusebius of Caesarea says that the disciples of Jesus cast lots to determine where each of them should go. Thomas was supposedly assigned to Parthia (now Iran and Iraq), Andrew to Scythia (now Ukraine), and John to the province of Asia Minor (now Turkey). Peter, as the group's leader, was given freedom to travel wherever he wanted.[1] Eusebius did not always get his facts straight and this particular story may well be a pious fiction, but his basic point is accurate. Within a century of Jesus's death, the Christian gospel had been exported far beyond the boundaries of Palestine, taking root as far west as Spain and as far east as India.

What exactly was this "gospel" or "good news" that the followers of Jesus sought to transmit around the world? Much of its content was derived from the teachings of Jesus himself: that God was humanity's dear father, that people were required to love each other, that repentance was the pathway to true righteousness, that ultimately everyone would stand before God and be judged, and that somehow Jesus's own suffering and death was part of God's plan to redeem humankind and the world. But Jesus himself never wrote any of this down; a literary legacy was not left behind. Jesus was not a writer, nor was he a systematic thinker or an institution builder. He was a storyteller who reveled in the spoken word. Later on, some of his followers recorded their memories of Jesus, preserving his teachings and the stories he told in short books called "gospels" (four of which are included in the New Testament). These accounts of Jesus's life and message do not, however, define the entirety of the gospel as Christianity proclaimed it.

The gospel *of* Jesus, what Jesus himself taught his followers, was quickly augmented within the Christian movement with a gospel *about* Jesus, a description of who Jesus was and why his life and teachings were so important. This gospel about Jesus proclaimed that he was more than merely human and more than merely one more prophet in a long line of Jewish prophets. He was the Messiah, a special and unique messenger from God, or perhaps he was even God incarnate. The Christian movement would later decisively emphasize the latter of these interpretations, but such a degree of clarity did not exist in the early decades. Everyone agreed, however, that Jesus was no mere mortal. He was the Christ (the anointed of God), and the gospel preached by his followers would ever after combine the message *of* Jesus of Nazareth with this additional message *about* Jesus the Christ.

Christianity's Original Diversity

During the first two centuries of its existence, Christianity remained a small religious movement with no discernible center or governing structure. Groups of Christians in different locations held widely varying opinions about almost every aspect of the movement, including who Jesus was, what salvation entailed, how the movement was related to Judaism, when and how the world would end, which sources of authority should guide the movement, and how the movement should be organized. The Bible had not yet been compiled, and institutional church structures were weak or nonexistent. It was a movement led by charismatic, often self-appointed, individuals who sometimes had conflicting visions for the movement's future. Even at the local level, Christians had their differences. In the Apostle Paul's first letter to the Corinthians, he indicates that many Christians in that city looked to a person named Apollos as their main guide and teacher, others looked to Peter, some followed Paul himself, and a few apparently claimed direct access to Christ with no need for any human teacher. Unanimity was clearly not the norm.

A short book called the *Didache* (meaning "teaching"), written around the year 100, advised early Christians about how to conduct themselves in this diverse and fluid environment. One immediate concern was evaluating the many wandering Christian prophets and preachers who traveled from town to town, providing instruction and seeking support from local Christian communities. The *Didache* says these peripatetic prophets should initially be welcomed as fellow believers, but they should be designated as false teachers if they stayed too long (more than two nights), if they asked for money or food, or if they failed to follow their own guidance. The document's advice on baptism is similarly practical and flexible. Instead of mandating one specific mode of baptism, the *Didache* says it is best to baptize individuals in a cold spring-fed stream, but if a stream is not available, then a cold lake or pool will do; if cold water cannot be found, then warm water is satisfactory; and if there is not enough water for full immersion, then pouring water over a person's head will suffice. Early Christianity was adaptable, and Christians felt little need to endorse just a single way of doing anything.[2]

Multiple versions of Christianity flourished alongside each other. Some Christian groups continued to insist that followers of Jesus needed functionally to become Jews and to obey the entirety of Jewish law. Other Christians adopted a position at the opposite extreme and condemned Judaism as thoroughly mistaken and evil. A person named Marcion, who grew up on the southern coast of the Black Sea and later moved to Rome, was the most prominent champion of this antisemitic perspective; he was also the first person to publish a collection of specially selected sacred Christian texts that prefigured the New Testament. Marcion's compilation included the Gospel of Luke, the book of Acts, and most of Paul's letters, but he removed anything in those texts that reflected favorably on Jews. Marcion and his antisemitic proto-New Testament were eventually rejected by the church in Rome where he was a member, but a separate Marcionite church continued to exist for several centuries. Another Christian group called the New Prophecy believed that God was still speaking directly to humankind through prophets whose words were as authoritative as those of Jesus. The movement was nominally led by a man named Montanus, but its prophetic oracles were both women, Prisca and Maximilla. Another significant subgroup of early Christians were called Gnostics, who delighted in formulating complex metaphysical descriptions of the universe and all the spiritual beings, both good and evil, that inhabit it. Gnostics claimed that Jesus had provided them with secret knowledge about how to negotiate their way through a complex and spiritually crowded universe after death and eventually make their way to heaven. The perspectives of Gnostics, Marcionites, members of the New Prophecy, and many others were all part of the early Christian amalgamation, and there was no central authority to adjudicate their conflicting claims.

Emergence of the Great Church

During the late second and early third centuries, a group of Christian bishops from the major cities of the Roman Empire launched a concerted effort to bring more structure, order, and male control to the movement. The immediate goal was to establish their own authority to govern the movement, and their proposals were based on a new theory called "apostolic succession." Apostolic succession operates along the same lines as a modern self-perpetuating board of trustees that chooses its own successors. For the early Christian movement, apostolic succession was established when Jesus selected his disciples and invested them with special authority to lead the movement in his post-ascension absence and when Christ's apostles then chose their successors and gave them special authority to lead the church. Those leaders subsequently had chosen their successors, and so on right up to the present day.

Bishops who could trace their lineage of leadership succession back to Jesus viewed themselves as having special authority within the movement and as having a special responsibility for imposing order on a movement that many of them considered to be much too freewheeling. Slowly these bishops formed themselves into a network of orthodox ("right-believing") Christian leaders who began establishing boundaries around their wing of the Christian movement, which they called the Great Church or simply the Church. Identifying heresy (wrong belief) became a focus of attention, and volumes with titles like *Against All Heresies*, written by Irenaeus who was bishop of the city of Lyon (France) from around 180 to 202, became standard texts for deciding who was in and who was outside the Great Church. Formal church membership now became a major concern, and Cyprian (208–258), the bishop of Carthage, bluntly declared that no one could "have God as Father who does not have the church as mother."[3] The bishops were never able to attract or corral everyone who called themselves followers of Jesus into the Great Church, but over time a majority of Christians became associated with their version of Christianity, and it developed into the mainstream of the movement.

There were advantages and disadvantages to Christianity's new organization and visibility. On the plus side, better organization helped the movement grow, since a standardized faith was easier to explain to others. On the negative side, persecution of Christians increased. Before 200, Christians in the Roman Empire were only occasionally subjected to persecution, primarily because the movement was too inconsequential to attract much attention. Once Christianity became better organized and more socially visible, Christians became useful scapegoats and popular targets for abuse. Persecution was especially intense between the years 250 and the early 300s when the Roman economy weakened and social unrest increased. It is estimated that five to ten thousand Christians were put to death during these years. That number represents less than 1 percent of all the Christians who lived in the empire at the time, but the executions were highly visible events – they were part of the "entertainment" that was staged in the colosseums and circuses in every Roman city – and having the courage willingly to die for one's faith became woven into the fabric of Christian identity.

The Roman Imperial Church

At the height of the worst persecution Christians had ever faced, a dramatic change took place. The Roman Emperor Constantine (who ruled from 306 to 337) converted to Christianity, and he halted the violence immediately. Soon he was actively favoring the Christian movement, and later in the century, under the rule of Theodosius I (379–395), Christianity as defined by the Great Church became the official religion of the Roman Empire.

It is difficult to assess the impact of Christianization on the empire as a whole, but the effect on the Christian movement itself was unquestionably substantial. Before Constantine, being a Christian involved personal risk. Suddenly, *not* being a Christian became a liability. Masses of people flocked into the movement, and the Christian population surged during the century following Constantine's conversion, catapulting from 10 or 15 percent of the Roman population to 75 percent or more. Accumulating more Christians is not equivalent, however, to developing better Christians, and there is some evidence that levels of religious piety and devotion decreased because people joined the movement out of convenience rather than out of conviction. The age of martyrdom also came to an end, and monasticism developed as a new way for individuals to express their complete devotion to God. Known as "white martyrs" (because no blood was involved), monks and nuns figuratively died to the world. Leaving their old lives behind, they fled to the desert where they could fully devote themselves to God with no earthly distractions.

Back in the world, as opposed to the desert, faith and politics were becoming ever more intertwined, and the institutional Great Church reaped the benefits. In 325, the Emperor Constantine himself called the bishops into council at Nicaea and charged them with developing a statement summarizing the core beliefs of true Christianity, so that every other alternative version of Christianity could be condemned and hopefully eliminated. Bishops from the Great Church readily agreed, and in doing so effectively turned the Great Church into the Imperial Church of the Roman Empire. The outcome of the council's work became known as the Nicene Creed, and it was used as a guide both in Christian worship and in identifying and persecuting other Christians who were deemed heretical. The Nicene Creed is still used as a statement of faith in many churches today.

Now able to operate freely in public with official support, the bishops of the Imperial Church increased their efforts to impose order and clarity on the Christian movement. One crucial task was to finalize the official canon (table of contents) of the New Testament. A number of different canons had been suggested over the years, but by the early 300s a consensus was beginning to emerge. The *Didache* (mentioned above) was one of the last documents to be eliminated from the New Testament list, and the book of Revelation (also known as the Apocalypse) was accepted only reluctantly because it was so susceptible to anti-imperial interpretation. The matter was firmly settled in the year 405 when the Palestinian monk and scholar Jerome (347–420) finished his Latin translation of the New Testament, and this text, known as the *Vulgate*, almost immediately became the definitive biblical text for most Christians. The New Testament used by the Persian Church had five fewer books (eliminating 2 Peter, 2 John, 3 John, Jude, and Revelation) and the Ethiopian New Testament had eight additional books, but most Christians of the time affirmed Jerome's twenty-seven-book canon.

With the approval and generous financial support of Roman authorities, Christians began building large and spectacular church buildings. Before the year 300, Christians had generally worshiped in relatively small quarters, often meeting in a house or similarly sized building. Once Christianity became the official religion of the empire, modest and provisional structures no longer seemed adequate or appropriate. New buildings were needed that could compete with or even outshine the grandeur of the older temples of Roman paganism, and enormous amounts of money were devoted to building massive, architecturally impressive church buildings called basilicas. As the architecture of the Christian movement changed, the visual art inside those buildings also changed. Most noticeably, Jesus got older and sterner. In the early centuries of Christianity, Jesus was typically pictured as a young, beardless shepherd carrying a lamb over his shoulders. The new portrayals typically depicted Jesus as a bearded, middle-aged judge or ruler on a throne (see Figure 1.1). Simultaneously, Christian worship became more elaborately choreographed, tailored to fit the magnificence of the new church buildings. Worship began to feel much more like an imperial court ritual than like a gathering of friends. Together, these changes signaled a major shift in Christian identity. Christianity was no longer the faith of social outcasts; it had become the faith of the prominent and powerful.

The Council of Chalcedon, held in the year 451, was intended to complete the Imperial Church's reorganization and its codification of correct beliefs. New guidelines regarding the behavior of monks/nuns and the clergy were announced, and the empire's churches were incorporated into a hierarchy headed by a handful of super-bishops called "patriarchs." The council also sought to end speculation about Christ's ontological identity. The Council of Nicaea in 325 had declared that Christ was both fully divine and fully human but

Figure 1.1 Figure of Jesus as a young shepherd (from the catacomb of Priscilla, Rome, third century) and Jesus as a middle-aged judge (from the Chora Church in Istanbul, originally constructed in the later fourth century). *Source*: Image on left: Joseph Wilpert, https://commons.wikimedia.org/wiki/File:Good_Shepherd_Catacomb_of_Priscilla.

had not explained how the two were related. Chalcedon declared that these human and divine *natures* were joined, but not merged, in the single *person* of Christ. This abstraction would have meant almost nothing to ordinary Christians, but it meant a great deal to the bishops and theologians of the Imperial Church because it gave them a firm standard for differentiating truth from error. It was also supposed to unify the Christian movement for all time. But it did not. Instead, the Chalcedonian Creed become a new flash point for division.

Christian Diversity and Unity in the Year 500

The Great Church in the Roman Empire was the largest group of Christians in the world when the Chalcedonian Creed was being written, but it was certainly not the only group. Many Christian sects (marginalized Christian communities that were not legally recognized by either the Imperial Church or the government of Rome) continued to survive out of public sight within the borders of the empire, and groups of Christians outside the Roman Empire were even more diverse. As early as the first century, Christianity had been introduced to southern India via maritime trade routes, and it subsequently became a permanent minority religion within India's complex social and spiritual environment. Christianity also put down roots in the Persian Empire (now Iraq and Iran) as early as the second century, and Christianity was brought to Armenia and Georgia in the Caucuses (the land between the Black Sea and the Caspian Sea) about the same time. Christianity made its way into Ethiopia during the fourth century, and later a group of nine theologically anti-Chalcedonian monks (known as the Nine Saints) fled south from Syria to Ethiopia where they helped to complete the evangelization of the region. Contemporaneously, Patrick was preaching the gospel in Ireland, where Christianity was organized along the lines of the Irish clan system rather than clustering around major urban centers as it did in the Roman Empire.

Christians adopted slightly different Christian identities in each separate region. Armenia, for example, was the first nation to officially embrace Christianity as its state religion, which remains a source of pride for Armenian Christians even today. Christians in Persia were severely persecuted – far beyond the horrors endured by Christians in the Roman Empire – but they remained faithful nonetheless, and joyful perseverance in suffering became a mainstay of their identity. In Ethiopia, where Judaism was historically respected, Jewish ideas and customs remained prominent in the movement. The fact that Christian communities adopted locally unique practices does not mean that they stopped thinking of themselves as belonging to a larger Christian movement that transcends cultural and national boundaries. Then, as now, Christians understood that being associated with a specific local Christian community was fully compatible with viewing other different Christians as siblings in faith. Christian unity was understood to be a matter of mutual recognition and respect much more than it was a matter of strict uniformity of practices or beliefs.

The Roman Imperial Church became the exception to this rule. Rome was a legalistic society, and the Roman Imperial Church imbibed that tendency toward legalism. Romans assumed that there really was one best and proper way to do everything, and the purpose of the law was to identify and enforce that one correct path. In earlier centuries, Christian communities had negotiated their way toward consensual agreements that mitigated conflict but simultaneously allowed reasonable differences to remain. This was true even of the Great Church before Constantine. As the church and the Roman state became more closely aligned, however, it became harder to maintain even a minimal degree of organizational graciousness. The Imperial Church wanted uniformity, and that desire eventually caused the larger Christian movement to snap under the pressure. A Great Division took place, and the formerly diverse but loosely connected Christian movement became three separate and distinct Christian traditions.

The Great Division

The Great Division took place during the first half of the sixth century, and it changed Christianity from being a complex religious movement into something more like a mosaic consisting of three separate and distinct ecclesiastical tiles. One of those tiles was the Roman Imperial Church, which continued to support the conclusions of the Council of Chalcedon. A second tile took shape in the Persian Empire, where the Church of the East emerged as a newly cohesive network of non-Roman congregations and monasteries. In between these two antagonistic empire-related Christian organizations, a third ecclesiastical coalition arose in Syria and Egypt, forming the third tile of Christianity's new mosaic. This third group is known as the Miaphysite tradition or Oriental Orthodoxy.

The Great Division is a watershed moment in the history of Christianity, not only because of the three new traditions that were created, but also because these three traditions soon came to dominate the entire Christian movement. Various independent, local Christian groups that had previously gone their own ways now felt compelled to choose sides. Christians in Georgia and Ireland, for example, chose to align with the Chalcedonian tradition, while Christians in Armenia and Ethiopia joined the Miaphysite movement. The consolidation of Christianity into three large and distinct communities, each nurturing its own tradition, permanently reshaped Christianity, and the space for smaller alternative visions of Christianity shrank to almost nothing (see Figure 1.2).

The flashpoint for the Great Division was Christology; the three groups held decidedly different views about who Jesus was and about the purpose of his life and death. Chalcedonians said that the human and divine natures were connected, but neither merged nor confused, in the one person of Christ. Miaphysites disagreed. They asserted that the human and the divine were fully merged and united in Christ, and they were convinced that salvation could

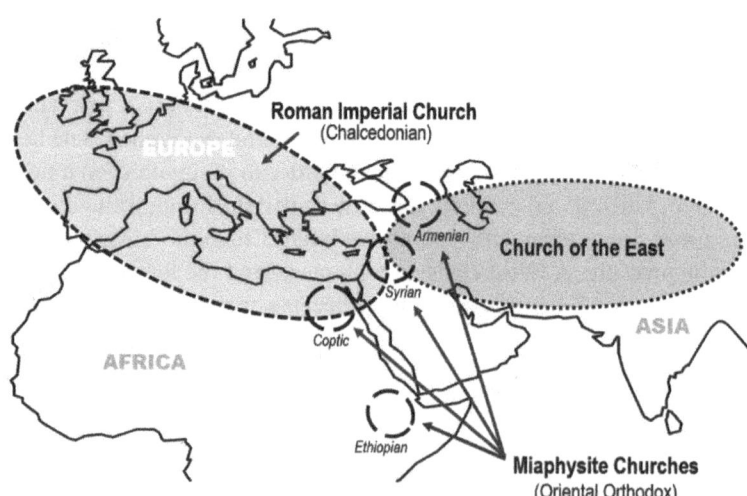

Figure 1.2 Geographic locations of the three traditions created by the Great Division.

occur only because God the Creator had literally felt the pain of death on the cross. It was God's full identification with the human condition, even to the point of death, that made salvation possible. The idea that God can experience emotions and fully understand the suffering of humankind is something that many modern Christians would agree with almost instinctively, but the Chalcedonian tradition (in opposition to the Miaphysite view) rejected this possibility, saying that God the Father was *apatheia* (non-feeling) and unmoved by earthly matters. For Chalcedonians, only an unchanging God had the power to guarantee eternal salvation, while Miaphysites believed that only a truly passionate God could and would try to save humankind.

Theological differences alone do not create a schism. Breaks as significant as the Great Division require an institutional component, as well, and that component was largely supplied by Jacob Baradeus (500–578), bishop of the city of Edessa (in what is now southern Turkey). During the middle of the sixth century, bishop Jacob traveled thousands of miles back and forth across the Middle East (both within and outside the Roman Empire) in order to ordain hundreds of priests and dozens of bishops to be part of a new Miaphysite church hierarchy standing in opposition to the Roman Imperial Church and the Chalcedonian beliefs it championed. Because of his efforts, the Miaphysite tradition (especially in Syria) is also known as the Jacobite Church. Non-Chalcedonian Christians in Egypt had established their own institutional independence even earlier under the leadership of a Miaphysite bishop called Timothy the Cat (d. 477). Miaphysite Christians living within the borders of the Roman Empire were sometimes subjected to brutal persecution by the Roman government (with the support and blessing of the Imperial Chalcedonian-oriented Church), which Miaphysite Christians interpreted as indisputable evidence that Chalcedonian Christianity was itself heretical. How, they asked, could any follower of Jesus condone such violence against other Christian believers when Jesus himself had commanded his disciples to love each other?

Meanwhile, the Church of the East tradition diverged from Chalcedon Christianity in the opposite direction from the Miaphysites. Instead of seeing Christ's personhood as a merger of the human and divine, Persian Christians stressed the separateness of the human and the divine in Christ. Persian Christians viewed ethics as central to Christian faith, and they accordingly viewed Jesus not only as a spiritual savior, but also as moral model for life. If Christ was to serve in this role, however – if Christ was to be seen as a realistic model for people to follow – he had to be fully and genuinely human and not somehow superhuman. One of the most well-known leaders of the Church of the East, the long-lived Catholicos Timothy I (728–823), made the argument that Christ had accomplished everything necessary for human salvation *before* his baptism by John in the River Jordan and that Christ remained on earth for three more years solely for the purpose of teaching his followers how they

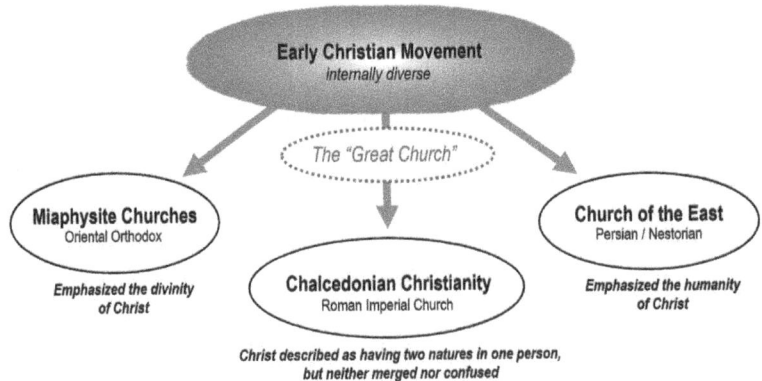

Figure 1.3 Diagram of the Great Division summarizing Christological differences.

should live. Christ's death on the cross was part of this instruction, and it showed Christians that they should not retaliate even when unjustly attacked by others. In contrast to Chalcedonians and Miaphysites who sometimes treated Christ's humanity almost as an afterthought, the Church of the East placed Christ's humanity at the center of their faith. (See Figure 1.3 for a summation of the Great Division and its Christological differences.)

The Church of the East was the most missionary-minded of the three traditions formed by the Great Division, and its missionary-monks spread the gospel all along the Silk Road, a series of ancient trade routes that meandered across Central Asia and connected China with the Middle East. The cities and towns that dotted the Silk Road tended to be religiously diverse, as trade centers often are, and Christians in this environment quickly ascertained that an embracing message of welcome was much more effective than criticizing other religions. Church of the East missionaries reached the Chinese capital city of Chang'an (known as Xi'an today) in the year 635. The Chinese emperor was deeply impressed by their positive message, which focused on Christ as a teacher and stressed the virtues of kindness and compassion. One Church of the East *sutra* (poetic sermon) from those years reads in part:

> Every being takes its refuge in You
> And the light of Your Holy Compassion frees us all...
> Great Teacher, I stand in awe of the Father.
> Great Teacher, I am awed by the Holy Lord.
> Great Teacher, I am speechless before the King of the Dharma.
> Great Teacher, I am dazzled by the Enlightened Mind –
> Great Teacher, you do everything to save us.
> Everything looks to You, without thinking.

Shower us with Your Healing Rain!
Help us to overcome, give life to what has withered,
And water the roots of kindness in us.[4]

The Chinese emperor dubbed Christianity the "religion of light," and he permitted the Church of the East to build monasteries wherever it desired. The Church of the East flourished in China until the mid-800s when China took a sudden xenophobic turn. Both Buddhist and Christian missionaries were expelled from the country, but Christianity seems to have been especially impacted, perhaps because the leadership of the movement remained mostly non-Chinese. Church of the East missionaries returned to China in the tenth century but never regained the prestige they formerly had enjoyed. Outside of China, the Church of the East maintained a significant presence in Persia and Central Asia until the fourteenth century when it finally withered under intense Muslim persecution.

The "Traditioning" of Christianity

The three traditions that emerged from the Great Division all saw themselves as legitimately tracing their roots back to Jesus, and each of them perceived their own beliefs and practices as a matchless effort to remain faithful to the gospel. All three groups continued to share a handful of beliefs and practices (for example, all of them believed God was a Trinity and all of them practiced the rites of baptism and the Eucharist), and a few genuinely exemplary individuals (like Isaac of Nineveh) were venerated as saints in all three traditions. However, their differences mattered. It was no longer possible to describe oneself simply as a Christian. After the Great Division, Christian identity required an adjective. You were a Chalcedonian Christian or a Miaphysite Christian or a member of the Church of the East, and it was no longer religiously meaningful to say one was simply a Christian without adding an additional signifier. To a large extent, this remains true today. The dominant Christian traditions have changed over the centuries, but the vast majority of Christians around the world continue to be affiliated with only a very few major traditions.

The root meaning of the word "tradition" is "to hand down," and Christian traditions are specific packages of religious beliefs, actions, and attitudes that have been handed down by a particular religious community from generation to generation. When some people hear the word "tradition," they equate it with "unchanging." For them, tradition represents the way things have always been, year after year, decade after decade; tradition is old fashioned and changeless. But this way of thinking is mistaken. Traditions evolve and grow, albeit often slowly, and handing anything down from generation to generation is a complicated and unpredictable process. In reality, religious traditions are long, multigenerational conversations which can involve a significant amount of argument and conflict. New generations add their own perceptions and concerns to the conversation, sometimes affirming and sometimes critiquing or revising what was done in the past, and older generations (and their contemporary supporters) are sometimes appalled, saddened, or infuriated by those changes. Occasionally, tensions become so great that communities feel compelled to divide, but usually some kind of compromise is reached, and the community moves forward together.

Over the course of the 1500 years since the Great Division, Christianity has been carried through history by only a handful of major traditions. In the year 650, the Christian world was dominated by the three traditions known as Chalcedonian, Miaphysite, and Church of the East. By the year 1100, the Chalcedonian tradition had divided in two, creating the separate and distinct Eastern Orthodox and Roman Catholic traditions. Five hundred year later, Catholicism and Orthodoxy had become Christianity's foremost traditions because the Church of the East had been persecuted into near oblivion and the Miaphysite churches had been severely reduced in size and influence, as well. Since 1500, the Catholic and Orthodox traditions have been joined by two other major Christian traditions: Protestantism, which began in the early 1500s, and Pentecostalism, which first took shape around 1900.

Currently, the Catholic tradition is home to roughly half the world's Christians, Orthodoxy serves about 10 percent of the total, and Protestantism and Pentecostalism split the rest with about 20 percent each. Taken together, these four contemporary traditions are embraced by roughly 97 percent of all Christians worldwide, so they are the logical places to begin answering the question "What is Christianity?" The next four chapters describe each of these traditions in detail, highlighting their spiritual and theological distinctives, tracing their divergent histories, and explaining their organizational structures. Whatever Christianity is today, almost all of it has been funneled down to the present through one or another of these traditions.

Notes

1 Eusebius of Caesarea, *Church History*, Book 3: Chapter 1, New Advent, https://www.newadvent.org/fathers/250103.htm (accessed August 27, 2020).

2 "The Didache," in Bart D. Ehrman ed., *Lost Scriptures: Books that Did Not Make It into the New Testament* (New York: Oxford University Press, 2005), pp. 211–219.

3 Cyprian, *On the Unity of the Church*, Christian History Institute, https://christianhistoryinstitute.org/study/module/cyprian (accessed August 27, 2020).

4 Martin Palmer, *The Jesus Sutras: Rediscovering the Lost Scrolls of Taoist Christianity* (New York: Ballantine, 2001), p. 166.

2

Orthodoxy

Preserving Ancient Ways

The Orthodox tradition preserves the ancient ideas and practices of Christianity more intentionally than any other tradition. In many ways, history is still alive in Orthodoxy, so much so that some outsiders view Orthodoxy as chained to the past. But for its adherents, Orthodox Christianity is still indisputably a living faith, a system of meaning and identity that connects them to the present and future as much as to the past.

Orthodox Christians have been socially marginalized and politically subjugated more than most Christians. Since the seventh century, many Orthodox Christians have lived in regions of the world ruled by Islamic governments where their religious rights have been limited. In the twentieth century, Orthodox Christians suffered greatly when Communists assumed control of Russia in 1917 and subsequently when Eastern Europe became Communist after World War II. This long history of social disempowerment, occasionally mixing with outright persecution, heightened their sense of group identity. Even today, being Orthodox is often a declaration of peoplehood as much as it is a personal affirmation of faith.

There are currently about 250 million Orthodox Christians in the world, constituting slightly more than 10 percent of the world's Christians. Orthodoxy is the smallest of the four traditions that dominate the Christian landscape today, and it is also the most geographically restricted. The original heartland of Orthodoxy was situated in what is now Turkey and the Middle East, but by 1500 the movement's demographic center had shifted north into Russia and Eastern Europe, which is where the majority of Orthodox Christians (more than 75 percent) now live.

Orthodox Spirituality

The spirituality of Orthodoxy focuses on worship, and to enter an Orthodox church is to enter a different place and time. Orthodox worship services are intended to give human beings a brief opportunity to participate in the eternal

What Is Christianity? First Edition. Douglas Jacobsen.

worship of God that is always taking place in heaven. Orthodox church buildings are designed to communicate this message. Many Orthodox churches have
domed ceilings, and at the top of the dome there is an opening called the *oculus*.
This is a symbolic eye into heaven. A huge picture of Christ as *Pantokrator* (the
ruler of all) is usually painted in the oculus, surrounded by angels and apostles,
looking down on the gathered congregation (see Figure 2.1). Orthodox worship
is like participating in an audience with God, and traditionally everyone stands
for the entire service as a way of showing respect to the Ruler of All. Some modern Orthodox churches have installed pews so people can sit down during worship, but many Orthodox Christians think this is inappropriate.

Orthodox Christians view the church building itself as sacred space, a temple
where God is uniquely present on earth. Other Christians sometimes refer to
their churches as "houses of God," but Orthodox Christians take the expression
more seriously than most. The Orthodox church floor plan is modeled after the
floor plan of the Jerusalem temple as described in the Hebrew scriptures (see
Figure 2.2), with the space for worshipers separated from the sanctuary by a
wall called an iconostasis (equivalent to the curtain that separated the holy
place from the holy of holies in the temple). The architecture of an Orthodox
church is meant to convey a sense of both holiness and mystery, and this sense

Figure 2.1 Holy Trinity Orthodox Cathedral (Sibiu, Romania), interior of main dome.

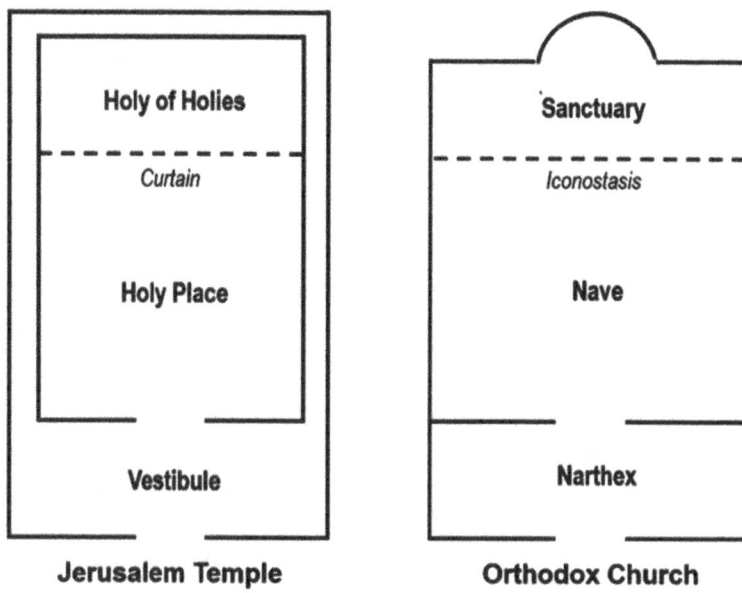

Holy of Holies	Sanctuary
Curtain	Iconostasis
Holy Place	Nave
Vestibule	Narthex
Jerusalem Temple	**Orthodox Church**

Figure 2.2 Floor plans of the ancient Temple in Jerusalem and a typical Orthodox Church showing similarity of layout.

of mystery is heightened in worship when the priest moves behind the iconostasis to the sanctuary and out of sight of worshipers in the nave when consecrating the Eucharist. Within the Orthodox tradition, the sacraments themselves are called "holy mysteries," rituals that draw people closer to God.

Most Orthodox churches are filled with religious paintings called icons. Icons are painted on the ceiling and walls of the building, icons hang from the iconostasis at the front of the nave, and icons appear on stands scattered throughout the building. Some icons portray Christ, Mary, the angels, and the great saints of the past. Other icons depict the stories of the Bible or important events in the history of Christianity. Icons play numerous roles within Orthodoxy, but their presence in churches is specifically meant to remind believers that they are not alone. Faith is lived in community, a community that persists through time and place and transcends even death. One is never alone, and nothing one does, whether in church or anywhere else, is ever done in secret. God is watching, Jesus is watching, Mary is watching, and the saints are watching too.

Orthodox iconography represents the world as Orthodox Christians believe it really exists behind the façade of ordinariness that people see with their physical eyes. Angels appear everywhere in icons because Orthodox Christians believe that angels are literally everywhere in reality. At baptism, Christians receive a guardian angel for protection from evil and for guidance in the ways of holiness, but fallen angels (demons) are also ubiquitously present, seeking to turn people away from God and faithfulness. Because this spiritual world is hidden from physical view, humans tend to forget that it is there. The liturgy and the icons remind people of this fact. The brilliant colors used in the painting of icons – and most of them were originally brilliant even though many old icons have grown dark with age – are luminous reminders that the spiritual world is as real, or more real, than the earth itself.

The most revered figure in the Orthodox tradition, apart from Jesus and the Holy Trinity, is Mary, who is called *Theotokos* ("God-bearer" or "Mother of God") because she bore God incarnate in her womb when she was pregnant with Jesus. Mary is venerated not only because she is the woman through whom God entered the world, but also because she models how every Christian should live. When the Archangel Gabriel told Mary that God had selected her to be *Theotokos*, she replied simply: "Let it be done to me, as I am your servant." Orthodox Christians believe that God comes to people gently offering life in its fullness and, like Mary, each person must respond. In addition to modeling obedience, Mary also models holy suffering, since she endured watching her son being crucified. Finally, she is considered the most compassionate of all the saints, and icons of Mary communicate her desire to comfort all those who seek help in times of pain and distress.

The prominence of the visual in Orthodox spirituality hints at Orthodoxy's distrust of words alone, and this distrust applies especially to theology. For most non-Orthodox Christians, "theology" refers to the philosophical analysis of Christian beliefs; it is about the words used to describe God, the world, and one's own salvation. For Orthodox Christians, "theology" is much more experiential. In its pure form, theology is the experience of living in God's holy presence. If words are deemed necessary to explain that experience, it is permissible to use them, but always reverently and with caution.

Orthodox Christians call their style of theology *apophatic*, an approach that accentuates the limited character of humanity's knowledge of God and the need for intellectual humility. Kallistos Ware, an Orthodox priest and longtime professor of Orthodox studies at Oxford University, likens apophatic theology to a person standing by a window at night and seeing lightning strike right next door. Reacting to the flash and thunderous blast, all that person can do is stagger backward in awe. Ware says that encountering "the living mystery of God" is like that. It is an experience beyond words and beyond the bounds of human knowing because God is so much greater than we are.[1] Orthodox Christians do not deny that there is a place for words and thought in Christian faith – a time for trying to explain the spiritual realities of life insofar as they can be translated into human discourse – but any theology of words is clearly secondary to theology as an experiencing of God.

From the Orthodox perspective, the highest and best theology is mystical communion with God that bypasses entirely the mediation of thoughts or ideas, and the only way to enter this kind of experience is through contemplation. The goal of contemplation is to clear the mind of all thoughts and distractions so that it becomes receptive to the divine. Contemplation takes time, which makes it a natural fit for the monastic life, but many laypeople also try to follow a way of life that involves continual prayer and longing for the presence of God. The most widely used method for attaining the stillness of mind that is needed to feel God's presence is the repetition of the "Jesus Prayer," which is also known as the "prayer of the heart." This short prayer consists of only twelve words: "Lord Jesus Christ, Son of God, have mercy on me, a sinner." Repeated almost inaudibly over and over again as individuals go about their daily activities, this prayer is intended to push away all worldly distractions and heighten spiritual acuity. The intention is that the prayer on one's lips will slowly become a genuine prayer of the heart, changing one's life and increasing one's awareness of God in the process.

Orthodox spirituality focuses on the higher world – the invisible world of God, the angels, and the saints – but that does not at all diminish Orthodoxy's regard for the natural world. Orthodox Christians believe the so-called natural world is infused with the supernatural. In fact, Orthodox Christians would say there is no such thing as a purely natural world, if "natural" is understood to mean somehow existing apart from God. All of creation is seen as holy. The current Ecumenical Patriarch Bartholomew has made this point – that the world is sacred and needs to be respected – so often that he is sometimes referred to as the "green patriarch." He argues that:

> We are treating our planet in an inhuman, godless manner precisely because we fail to see it as a gift inherited from above. Our original sin with regard to the natural environment lies in our refusal to accept the world as a sacrament of communion, as a way of sharing with God and neighbor on a global scale. It is our humble conviction that divine and human meet in the slightest detail contained in the seamless garment of God's creation, in the least speck of dust.[2]

For Orthodox Christians God is in and around everything, sanctifying reality. This means, among other things, that ordinary human life is seen as good and meant to be enjoyed. Time together with family and friends is considered a blessing, and the church itself becomes a kind of extended family. Living together in the fellowship of the church requires periods of fasting, but it also requires times to party and feast. There are occasions for repentance and sorrow, but also for celebration, including the enjoyment of good food and wine. Rather than conflicting with the other-worldly emphases of Orthodox spirituality, this earthly spirituality grounds it in the here and now. Orthodox spirituality is deeply life-affirming and nurtures an awareness that all of life is lived in God's holy presence.

The Orthodox Understanding of Salvation

Orthodoxy holds a view of salvation that is broad and expansive. Instead of focusing primarily on an individual's personal reconciliation with God, salvation is construed as something that happens to people in groups. Orthodox Christians often say that no one is saved alone, but only in community. Also, the goal of salvation is more than mere reconciliation with God and other human beings. The desired outcome is *theosis*, the "deification" or divine transformation of individuals, of humankind as a whole, and ultimately of all creation. In keeping with this broad and active sense of *theosis*, Orthodox Christians would never claim that they have been *saved* in the past tense. Instead, salvation is always active and ongoing, a process that continually draws one further and deeper into communion with God and others. Orthodox Christians might say they are, by God's grace, on the path toward salvation or that they are being saved, but no one expects to experience the fullness of salvation in this lifetime.

Words like *theosis* and deification are jarring to many people who are not themselves Orthodox Christians. The notion of deification is meant to be jarring; its claim is stunning. Orthodox Christians often say that God became human so that humans could become divine. In this way of thinking about salvation, it is Christ's incarnation that takes center stage, instead of the death of Christ. God enters human lives, and in response human beings enter deeper and deeper into unifying fellowship with the Trinitarian God who is the great lover of the world and everyone in it. The eighth-century Orthodox theologian Manşūr ibn Sarjūn (also known as John of Damascus) explained it this way: "Those who, through their own choice and the indwelling and cooperation of God, have become assimilated to God as much as possible...are truly called gods, not by nature, but by adoption, as iron heated in the fire is called fire, not by nature, but by its condition and participation in fire."[3]

The image in this description is one of God as fire and of the deified person as a piece of iron that has become bright red through contact with the fire of God. This image communicates both the otherness of God's holiness and also Orthodox theology's generally positive view of human nature, which is significantly more optimistic than what typically appears in either Catholic or Protestant theology. Rather than seeing people as totally lost and overcome by sin, Orthodoxy sees humans as merely weakened by sin in much the same way that sickness weakens people physically. Salvation is less like total transformation than it is like regaining strength after being sick. In fact, the consecrated bread and wine of Orthodox worship are sometimes described as "the medicine of immortality," which strengthens people for the spiritual journey that takes them back to God. Going back to Manşūr's imagery, the iron remains iron just as human beings remain human beings, but the fiery glow of God's presence strengthens them and makes them conduits of grace for others.

God's presence in anyone's life is an expression of God's love not just for that individual, but for everyone in the world and indeed for the entire universe. To be truly aglow with God's presence is to be filled with God's love for everyone and everything, so that focusing on one's own individual salvation becomes unthinkable. Salvation reverses the human propensity to see the world in terms of self versus others.

The breadth of Orthodoxy's vision of salvation raises the question of universal salvation: Will everyone without exception eventually be saved? The technical term for this kind of universal salvation is *apokatastasis*. Some Orthodox church leaders and synods have condemned *apokatastasis*, arguing that evil humans who reject God's grace will, like the demons, be damned forever. But others, including some of the most respected theologians in the history of the Orthodox tradition like Gregory of Nyssa (fourth century) and Maximus the Confessor (seventh century), argue that everyone, even the demons, will eventually be restored to fellowship with God.

Such debates are far removed from the personal journeys toward salvation of most Orthodox Christians. Their journeys begin with baptism, when a baby is welcomed into fellowship with God and others in the church. The fact that the recipients of baptism are infants who are unable to do anything for themselves underscores that God's grace always comes as a gift. No one earns it. In the act of baptism a baby receives a new life beyond the merely physical; it marks the beginning of a new spiritual relationship with parents, with the godparents who are part of the ceremony, with everyone who is already in the church, with the child's guardian angel, with Christ, and with the entirety of the Holy Trinity. As children mature, they must slowly own their baptism for themselves, but they are not beginning from scratch. Even adult converts start midway because others have helped them in their journey of faith. No one comes to God alone.

Assisted by others to enter the path of salvation – a pathway that is itself an unmerited gift from God – Orthodox Christians believe their own effort is necessary in order for progress to continue. There are two parts to this effort: first, sorrowing for the willful sin discovered in one's own life and, second, persisting in the practice of prayer by learning to push all earthly thoughts and cares of life aside in order to simply *be* in the presence of God. But these efforts are never individualistic. It is primarily in worship with others that a person learns how to pray, and it is by feeding together on the bread and wine of the Eucharist – which is given even to children – that a person receives spiritual sustenance for continuing the journey toward salvation in the company of others.

Orthodox History

Orthodox Christians trace the roots of their tradition back through the ancient Roman Empire to Christ himself. This history includes the Council of Nicaea (325), the Council of Chalcedon (451), and the Great Division that took place in the sixth century. The Orthodox tradition remains proudly grounded in the conclusions of these early councils and retains its Chalcedonian allegiance. Orthodoxy is, however, more than mere Chalcedonianism, and part of its identity is linguistic. The Roman Empire was bilingual, with Latin spoken in the West and Greek in the East, and Orthodoxy emerged out of the Greek-speaking side of this divide. In the 400s, the Roman Empire became politically divided along these same lines when the western half of the empire was conquered by Germanic (barbarian) tribes. The remaining eastern half of the old Roman Empire then reorganized itself as the Byzantine Empire, and the Christianity that flourished in this new Greek-speaking empire slowly morphed into Orthodoxy as we know it today.

The Expansion and Consolidation of Orthodoxy in Byzantium, 500 to 900

The Byzantine Empire (or Byzantium as it was often called) was an explicitly Christian domain, and most Byzantine Christians believed that their empire represented the beginning of the Kingdom of God on earth. They assumed that Christ's rule over Byzantium would slowly extend over the whole world, and they believed that their capital, the city of Constantinople, protected by the Virgin Mary, would forever remain the center of God's kingdom on earth. This attitude of imperial Christian power provides the background for understanding Orthodoxy's expansive vision of salvation. The most articulate spokesperson for this newly magnified view of salvation was Maximus (580–662), who was also known as "the Confessor" because of his perseverance under persecution by the heretical (in the eyes of Orthodox Christians) Emperor Heraclius.

Maximus argued that the unique connection between the human and the divine in Christ (united, but not merged or confused) that had been developed by the Council of Chalcedon was the key for understanding reality as a whole. Taking a cue from the Apostle Paul's proclamation that God would someday unite all things in heaven and earth in Christ (Ephesians 1:9–10), Maximus proposed that the creation and the Creator were already united as a result of the Incarnation. In this union, the created world remained the created world and God remained God – the divine and the non-divine were never merged or confused with each other – but somehow these two dimensions of reality became connected. Though presently visible only through the eyes of faith, the full cosmic "mystery of Christ" eventually will be revealed for all to see.[4] The Orthodox tradition cannot be understood apart from this grand vision of God's presence in, and future redemption of, the entire creation – a cosmic vision befitting a Christian Empire.

This very same belief – that creation and the Creator can be and somehow already are mystically connected – animated another decisive moment in Orthodox history known as the Iconoclastic Controversy. Viewed narrowly, this was a dispute over the question of whether it is ever appropriate to venerate pictures of Christ and the saints. The deeper issue was whether the stuff of creation, things like paint and wood, could be carriers of God's holiness in the world. The dispute began in the year 726. The Byzantine Empire had lost considerable territory to the rapidly growing Islamic Caliphate, and Emperor Leo III thought that God must be punishing the empire for some heinous sin. He eventually decided that icons were the source of the problem. The second of the Ten Commandments forbids the making and worship of images (Exodus 20:4–6) and, determining that the veneration of icons transgressed this commandment, Leo banned them.

Many ordinary believers and church leaders were appalled by Leo's attack on icons, and they fought back. They loved these holy images and were sure that pictures of Christ and the saints had helped them in times of worry and need. A long-running dispute ensued, pitting *iconophiles* (lovers of icons) against the emperor and his *iconoclastic* supporters. No one was more articulate in providing a rationale for the love of icons than the Orthodox monk and theologian Manşūr ibn Sarjūn, who argued that the veneration of icons was not only allowable but essential. For him, denying the efficacy of icons amounted to denying God's promise of salvation:

> In former times God, who is without form or body, could never be depicted. But now when God is seen in the flesh conversing with men, I make an image of the God whom I see. I do not worship matter; I worship the Creator of matter who became matter for my sake, who willed to take His abode in matter; who worked out my salvation through matter.[5]

The Second Council of Nicaea, convened by the Empress Irene and held in the year 787, sought to end the controversy partly by making a strict differentiation between the legitimate *veneration* of icons and the act of true worship or *adoration* which was reserved for God alone. Not everyone was convinced, however, and some iconoclasts continued their anti-icon efforts. Finally, in 843, another Byzantine Empress, Theodora, organized another synod of bishops to reaffirm the importance of icons. Theodora put the full weight of the Byzantine government behind the council's pronouncement, and the iconoclast movement collapsed. Aptly known as the "Triumph of Orthodoxy," Theodora's intervention insured that icons would play a central role in Orthodox faith ever after, and this development marks the coming of age of Orthodoxy as a distinct and unique Christian tradition. As if to confirm this transition, Orthodox Christians around the world celebrate this event every year on the first Sunday in Lent, and it feels almost like a birthday celebration for the Orthodox tradition.

Orthodoxy in a Slowly Faltering Empire, 900 to mid-1400s

As early as the mid-seventh century, the Byzantine Empire had begun to falter under military pressure from the ever-expanding Muslim world. The Macedonian dynasty, which ruled Byzantium from 867 to 1025, managed to stabilize the empire, but when Macedonian rule ended things began to fall apart. The Battle of Manzikert (in 1071) is often cited as the turning point initiating Byzantium's inexorable decline into oblivion. As political confidence waned and as Byzantium's self-identification with the Kingdom of God on earth became increasingly implausible, Byzantine faith itself changed. Maximus's cosmic vision of God's plan for the world became less resonant and the personal dimensions of faith acquired new appeal and significance.

A monk named Symeon (949–1022) articulated a rationale for Orthodoxy's turn toward personal faith. Symeon is often called "the New Theologian." Only two Orthodox leaders before him had been honored with the title of theologian, which signaled respect for the depth of their personal experience of God's presence, and God's presence was central to Symeon's own message. He declared that passionate encounters with God like those described so effusively by the early mothers and fathers of the Orthodox Church could still be experienced in the present. He knew this to be true because he had experienced it himself, talking with God "as friend speaks to friend face to face."[6] At first, Byzantine Orthodox leaders condemned his views, because they saw God as much too lofty to participate in any cozy, face-to-face conversations with human beings. But eventually their opinions changed, and Orthodoxy adopted Symeon's views. If salvation is a slow process of *theosis*, then it seems reasonable to conclude that it ought to involve at least some awareness of the divine presence in one's life.

Symeon's emphasis on religious experience inspired Orthodox monks to develop practices of prayer that fostered these kinds of divine experiences. One popular technique of prayer and meditation was called *hesychasm*, meaning stillness or quietude. Hesychasts were known for praying the Jesus Prayer in a yoga-like manner, breathing in while reciting part of the prayer and breathing out when finishing it. Practitioners claimed this technique allowed them to still their souls sufficiently for the "uncreated light" of God to become visible, an experience that they deemed to be the equivalent of Symeon's speaking with God face-to-face. Once again critics raised questions, and some of them condemned hesychasts for over-hyping the closeness of their relationship with God.

Another Orthodox monk came to the rescue. Gregory Palamas (1296–1359) suggested that hesychasts were not seeing God in God's fullness. He agreed that no person could do so and remain alive. Instead, hesychasts were seeing the *energies* of God in contrast to God's *essence* itself. Gregory based this interpretation of the hesychastic experience on the New Testament story of Christ's transfiguration on Mt. Tabor when the disciples saw Jesus transformed with his face as bright as the sun and his clothes white as light (Matthew 17:1–2). This new theology regarding the energies of God gave Orthodox Christians a way to explain how one could have a direct and personal interaction with God, while simultaneously preserving the notion that God in Godself was *apatheia* (passionless) and unchangeable. In a faltering empire when many other certainties were waning, the dual assurance that God was both personal and changeless was tremendously reassuring.

As the Orthodox tradition continued to refine its beliefs and practices, it became ever more apparent that Orthodoxy was a different kind of Chalcedonian-based Christianity than the Catholicism (also Chalcedonian-based) that was developing in Western Europe. These differences erupted in 1054 when leaders of the two traditions mutually condemned each other, and the East–West schism that separated Orthodoxy from Catholicism has persisted ever since. An additional layer of bitterness was added in 1204 when Western Catholic crusaders on their way to fight Muslims in the Holy Land instead attacked the city of Constantinople and tried to force Orthodox Christians to become Catholic. Even more enmity was created by the Council of Florence (mid-1400s) which pressured a few Byzantine Orthodox leaders into acknowledging the spiritual authority of the pope. Submission to the Catholic pope was vehemently and immediately rejected by the Orthodox movement as a whole, and the attempted takeover further increased distrust of Catholicism.

Orthodoxy After the Fall of Byzantium, 1453 to the Present

Shortly after the Council of Florence, the Byzantine Empire collapsed. The city of Constantinople surrendered to the Ottoman sultan on May 29, 1453, and Orthodoxy entered a new phase in its history. The Ottoman Empire continued to expand northward into Eastern Europe, and a majority of the world's Orthodox population was soon living under Muslim rule. As a result, Russia (which at the time was a free and independent Christian nation after emerging from two centuries of Islamic Mongol dominance) became the new geographic and political center of Orthodoxy. Orthodoxy had been introduced to Russia in the late 900s, and it flourished in its new setting. Russian Orthodox Christians were adamantly Orthodox, and they were appalled by Byzantium's capitulation to Catholicism at the Council of Florence. It seemed obvious to Russians that their own country had been much more faithful to Orthodoxy than Constantinople, and the Patriarch of Moscow began to claim that God had made him (and his office) the highest-ranking bishopric within the Orthodox world. This perspective is still embraced by many Russian Orthodox Christians today.

However, the Russian Orthodox Church was soon confronting internal problems of its own. In the mid-1600s, the Russian Orthodox Church experienced a bitter split over the Orthodox liturgy, with Old Believers (also known as Old Ritualists) taking a conservative stance against innovations introduced by the Patriarch Nikon (in office 1652–1666).When Nikon altered a handful of elements within the liturgy, the Old Believers promptly left the Church. Their descendants, called *raskolniki* (schismatics or "splitters"), continue to worship apart from the mainstream Orthodox Church in Russia today. Shortly after this schism and partly to avoid similar divisions in the future, Tsar Peter the Great (in office 1682 to 1725) abolished the Russian Orthodox Patriarchate and placed the church under direct government control through the office of the Ober-Procurator. With passing generations, Russian Orthodoxy became ever more parochially Russian. Birthday celebrations of the tsars and other members of the royal family became national religious holidays, older pagan religious celebrations continued with only a thin veneer of Orthodoxy to Christianize them, and local saints and holy sites became ever more important to Russian Orthodox spirituality. Amid disruptions associated with World War I, the Russian Tsar Nicholas II resigned from office in 1917 and, during the political vacuum that ensued, a council of Russian Orthodox Church leaders was convened and voted to restore the patriarchate. Almost simultaneously, however, Communists took control of the government, and Russian Orthodox Christianity entered a long period of intense persecution during the years when Russia was merged into the larger Union of Soviet Socialist Republics.

After seven decades of despotic Communist rule, the Union of Soviet Socialist Republics dissolved in 1991, and Russia once again became its own separate nation. The new post-Communist Russian government has been overwhelmingly supportive of the Orthodox Church, and the turnaround has been stunning. The Russian state (and President Vladimir Putin in particular) is now the great defender of Orthodoxy, and the Orthodox Church has, in turn, become an ardent defender of the Russian state and President Putin. Being ethnically Russian and being Orthodox have become almost synonymous, and church and state work hand-in-hand to limit the influence of any non-Orthodox churches in the country. The Russian people remain steadfastly committed to Orthodoxy, and Russian Orthodoxy continues to exercise enormous influence within the larger Orthodox world.

Orthodox Christians in the Balkans and Eastern Europe, unlike those in Russia, lived under Muslim rule as part of the Ottoman Empire for many generations during the sixteenth through the early nineteenth centuries. The

Ottomans grouped all Orthodox Christians together into one *dhimmi* (a minority religious population unit) under the authority of the Patriarch of Constantinople, and non-Greek Orthodox communities, especially the Serbs and Bulgarians, chaffed at their loss of religious independence. Searching for support and resources, some Orthodox leaders turned toward the West for help and inspiration. At least one Ecumenical Patriarch (Cyril Lucaris) was drawn to ideas of the Protestant reformer John Calvin; others were attracted to Protestant Pietism's emphasis on personal faith; and some even adopted Catholic views or became formally Catholic themselves, seeking a more realistic, less idealistic view of sin, salvation, and the created order. Because non-Orthodox ideas became so influential during these years, some Orthodox historians now refer to this period as a time of "Western Captivity" in addition to being a time of subjugation to Islam.

Independence began to return to Orthodoxy in Eastern Europe and the Balkans in the nineteenth century as the Ottoman Empire slowly weakened and withdrew from Europe (see Figure 2.3). Restoration of political independence and ecclesiastical independence often proceeded in unison. Sometimes political independence came first. This was the case in Greece, where political independence was restored in 1832, ecclesiastical autonomy (partial independence) was claimed in 1833, and autocephalous status (full church independence) was granted by the Patriarch of Constantinople in 1850. For other nations, such as Romania, ecclesiastical independence came first (1865), followed by national independence in 1877, and full autocephaly in 1925.

This new flourishing of nation-defined Orthodoxy raised questions about just how closely related church and state ought to be. Orthodox Christianity has a long history of distinguishing between proper cooperation with the state (called

Figure 2.3 Simplified map of Eastern Europe showing national boundaries in 1700 and 1900.

symphonia) and improper veneration of, or subservience to, the state (called *phyletism*). The line between *symphonia* and *phyletism* has not always been evident to church leaders, however. During the Balkan Wars of the 1990s (following the dissolution of Yugoslavia), for example, some leaders of the Serbian Orthodox church were accused of supporting policies of ethnic cleansing directed against Catholics and Muslims, a malignant outgrowth of their desires to strengthen and enlarge the Orthodox Serbian state.

The Ecumenical Patriarch continues to reside in the old city of Constantinople (now called Istanbul), and his freedom is restricted to some degree by the Turkish state. Living in a nation where Christians represent only a tiny fraction of the population, the patriarch is perhaps ideally situated to understand the dangers of religious alliances with the state. He is also living in a country where Christians have sometimes been severely persecuted, as with the Armenian genocide that took place in the early twentieth century and the deportation of a million Greek Orthodox Christians in the 1920s. Rather than touting the virtues of religious nationalism, the Ecumenical Patriarch Bartholomew has instead warned against hyper-nationalism and the racism that often accompanies it, calling it one of the gravest threats to Orthodoxy worldwide. In early 2020, he wrote:

> It is absolutely forbidden for Christians to make an idol of cultural, ethnic, or national identity. There can be no such thing as a "Christian nationalism," or even any form of nationalism tolerable to Christian conscience. ...[I]n much of the developed world [there is a resurgence] of the most insidious ideologies of identity, including belligerent forms of nationalism and blasphemous philosophies of race. ...There could be no greater contradiction of the Gospel [than this]. There is only one human race, to which all persons belong.[7]

Orthodoxy's nationalist and self-protective attitudes may be understandable given its long history of being oppressed, but the Ecumenical Patriarch seems to have a broader view of what Orthodoxy is and can be. Orthodoxy takes pride in having remained true to the faith through hard times, and it remains committed to continuity with the past. However, in recent centuries the Orthodox tradition has dwindled more than any other tradition. Orthodoxy accounted for about 30 percent of all Christians in 1800; by 1900 that number had fallen to about 20 percent, and today Orthodox Christians constitute only slightly more than 10 percent of all Christians worldwide. If Orthodoxy is to remain one of Christianity's major traditions, it may need to follow the Ecumenical Patriarch by rethinking some of its ethnic inclinations and embracing a broader sociological vision of what Orthodoxy can be.

Institutional and Social Structure of Orthodoxy

Sometimes reference is made to the Orthodox Church in the singular. While it is true that all Orthodox Christians see themselves as spiritual members of God's one church on earth, there is no single institutional entity that can be identified as "the Orthodox Church." Instead, the Orthodox tradition is housed in a network of related nationally defined churches that exist in fellowship with each other, and each of those separate churches possesses one of three levels of self-governance. Some of these churches are fully independent and are therefore called "autocephalous," which literally means "self-headed." The leader of an autocephalous Orthodox Church is typically called a patriarch. At present there are fourteen undisputed autocephalous Orthodox churches worldwide. Other Orthodox churches, usually smaller churches that would find it difficult to exist on their own, are "autonomous" in the sense that they generally run their own affairs, but they are technically under the supervision of some fully autocephalous church. For example, the Orthodox Church of Finland, while largely independent, is technically an archdiocese of the Church of Constantinople. Similarly, the Orthodox Church of Japan is governed by a metropolitan (roughly equivalent to archbishop) who reports to the Patriarch of Moscow. Finally, there is a third group of Orthodox churches whose varying claims of independence have not yet been fully settled. Table 2.1 lists most of the Orthodox churches in the world and indicates their current ecclesiastical status.

The various churches that together constitute the Eastern Orthodox tradition have a distinctive interpretation of their interconnectedness. Their ties are organic, mystical, and almost biological, in contrast to what they see as the institutional and legalistic bonds of Catholicism or the merely associational connections among Protestants and Pentecostals. The Orthodox tradition believes its group identity is so unique that they have developed a special vocabulary to describe it, using terms like synodality, conciliarity, and *sobornost* (fellowship). Taking these ideals a step further, some Orthodox leaders are now championing a pan-Orthodox understanding of faith, hoping to further improve communication and cooperation among all the world's different Orthodox churches.

At present, however, any and all notions of Orthodox unity are being challenged by a massive rift between the patriarchs of Constantinople and Moscow, the two most important Orthodox leaders in the world. The main bone of contention focuses on "canonical territory." In the early Christian movement, it was generally assumed that each major city or region of the Roman Empire would have one and only one bishop. Within Orthodoxy, this principle was generalized to forbid any Orthodox church from interfering in the

Table 2.1 Major Eastern Orthodox Churches with current ecclesiastical status and estimated membership.

Church	Ecclesiastical status (date of autocephaly)	Estimated membership
Orthodox Church of Albania	autocephalous (1937)	500,000
Orthodox Church of Alexandria	autocephalous (381)	500,000
Orthodox Church in America	claims autocephaly, but disputed	100,000
Orthodox Church of Antioch	autocephalous (381)	4,000,000
Orthodox Church in Belarus	divided / part claims independence; part is under the jurisdiction of Moscow	5,500,000
Orthodox Church of Bulgaria	autocephalous (1961)	6,000,000
Orthodox Church of Constantinople	autocephalous (381)	5,000,000
Orthodox Church of Cyprus	autocephalous (431)	500,000
Orthodox Church of Czech Lands and Slovakia	autocephalous (1951)	100,000
Orthodox Church in Estonia	divided / part claims independence; part is under the jurisdiction of Moscow	150,000
Orthodox Church of Finland	autonomous / under jurisdiction of Constantinople	60,000
Orthodox Church of Georgia	autocephalous (466)	3,500,000
Orthodox Church of Greece	autocephalous (1850)	10,000,000
Orthodox Church of Japan	autonomous / under jurisdiction of Moscow	10,000
Orthodox Church of Jerusalem	autocephalous (451)	500,000
Orthodox Church of Latvia	autonomous / under the jurisdiction of Moscow	400,000
Orthodox Church of Macedonia	claims autonomy / not recognized	1,300,000
Orthodox Church in Moldova	divided / part under the jurisdiction of Moscow; part under jurisdiction of Romania	4,000,000
Orthodox Church of Montenegro	claims autonomy / not recognized	150,000
Orthodox Church of Poland	autocephalous (1948)	500,000
Orthodox Church of Romania	autocephalous (1925)	18,000,000
Orthodox Church of Russia	autocephalous (1589)	110,000,000
Orthodox Church of Serbia	autocephalous (1346)	7,500,000
Orthodox Church of Sinai	disputed / either autonomous or autocephalous	<100
Orthodox Church in Ukraine	divided / part claims independence; part under the jurisdiction of Moscow	32,000,000

territorial jurisdiction of any other Orthodox church. Currently, the Russian Orthodox Church claims authority over Orthodoxy in Estonia and Ukraine, but the Patriarch of Constantinople has intervened in both regions, supporting Orthodox subgroups that want to remove themselves from Russian control. Russian Orthodox leaders perceive this to be a blatant transgression of canonical territory, and in response have severed their ties with Constantinople. While circumstances could change, there is currently little hope for reconciliation between these two Orthodox superpowers.

All the world's Orthodox Churches are organized in roughly the same way. The *see* or diocese, which is governed by a bishop, is the basic geographic unit of organization. Bishops of larger territories and important cities are sometimes given different titles like archbishop, metropolitan, catholicos, or patriarch as signals of honor, but all Orthodox bishops are technically spiritual equals. Unlike the Catholic Church which has one pope, there is no overall head of the Orthodox Church. Historically, the Ecumenical Patriarch of Constantinople holds honorary first place among Orthodox bishops, but this place of honor confers none of the authority wielded by the Catholic pope. Orthodox bishops, like Catholic bishops, are expected to be celibate, and most of them were previously monks. The transition from monastery to diocese is usually not very difficult, however, because Orthodox monks regularly interact with laypeople and sometimes serve as their spiritual advisors. Small monasteries are scattered throughout the Orthodox world, often in or near cities and towns, and Orthodox laypeople make frequent visits. Orthodox women can also become monastics, but Orthodox women cannot become bishops or priests.

In contrast to the bishops (and in contrast to Catholicism), most Orthodox priests are married. In fact, that is the preference. The family is central to Orthodox Christianity, and it is assumed that a good priest will provide sound and realistic advice to married parishioners, something that might be awkward for unmarried men. The Orthodox refer to the family as "the little church," the place where children first learn about God and where everyone experiences the joys and difficulties of living in close-knit community. Orthodox church buildings reflect this familial ethos. While the Orthodox churches that tourists visit are usually large and impressive structures, many Orthodox churches are small and intimate (see Figure 2.4). A local village or neighborhood church may accommodate only fifteen or twenty people, and frequently every worshiper in the room will be related by blood or marriage to everyone else.

Orthodoxy has been a family religion for many centuries. It has been genealogical, a way of life passed down from generation to generation. A person who is born into an Orthodox family will find it is very hard to become non-Orthodox. People can stop believing in God and never go to church, yet they will still be considered Orthodox by family and friends, and probably even by themselves.

Figure 2.4 Interior of small Orthodox church (Cyprus).

In more recent years, Orthodoxy (especially outside of Europe) has begun attracting significant numbers of converts. These converts have no interest in changing Orthodox beliefs or its worship style, because that is what attracts them to Orthodoxy. However, some converts are challenging Orthodoxy's ethnic practices. As one convert explains: "When I became Orthodox I didn't become Russian, Finnish, or Serbian. I'm here for the faith, not the pierogis; I don't know how to do Greek dancing or paint Ukrainian eggs."[8]

Even as it absorbs newcomers, Orthodoxy is working hard to maintain its powerful customs of connectedness. The Orthodox tradition not only connects people to God, it also connects them to each other, to the past, to the saints and angels in heaven, and to the entirety of the created world. All those connections provide a welcome sense of belonging in a world where so many people feel socially and spiritually adrift. As a tradition, Orthodoxy simultaneously emphasizes God's immensity and mystery and God's intimacy and closeness. God is presented as greater than any human being can possibly comprehend, but also closer and more caring than any friend or loved one. Orthodoxy de-centers the self. If Orthodoxy says anything clearly, it is that salvation is not all about you. Personal salvation is embedded in God's larger, grander work in the world. An individual is spiritually healed and redeemed only because everyone and everything around them is being healed and redeemed simultaneously. In an age when so much stress is placed on personal authenticity – on being oneself without interference or assistance from anyone else – Orthodoxy offers a respite. There is no need to blaze your own way; Orthodoxy allows individuals to relax into community and to follow pathways of faith that have been worn smooth by the footfalls of many previous generations.

Notes

1 Kallistos Ware, *The Orthodox Way* (Crestwood, NY: St. Vladimir's Seminary Press, 1979), p. 13.
2 Ecumenical Patriarch Bartholomew of Constantinople, "Environmental Justice and Peace," https://www.orthodoxcouncil.org/-the-green-patriarch- (accessed June 10, 2020).
3 John of Damascus, *Three Treatises on the Divine Images*, translated by Andrew Louth (Crestwood, NJ: St. Vladimir's Seminary Press, 2003), p. 106.
4 Maximus, *On the Cosmic Mystery of Jesus Christ: Selected Writings from Maximus the Confessor*, translated by Paul M. Bowers and Robert Louis Wilken (Crestwood, NY: St. Vladimir's Seminary Press, 2003).
5 John of Damascus, *Three Treatises on the Divine Images*, p. 23.
6 Symeon the New Theologian, *The Discourses*, translated by C.J. deCatanzaro (Mahwah, NJ: Paulist Press, 1980), p. 365.
7 Ecumenical Patriarch Bartholomew of Constantinople, "For the Life of the World: Toward a Social Ethos of the Orthodox Church," (January 18, 2020) online at https://www.goarch.org/social-ethos (accessed April 25, 2020).
8 Frederica Mathewes-Green, *At the Corner of East and Now: A Modern Life in Ancient Christian Orthodoxy* (New York: Putnam, 1999), p. 10.

3

Catholicism

The Church

The Catholic tradition is the largest of Christianity's four main traditions, as it has been for centuries. With more followers than the other three traditions combined, Catholicism continues to dominate the Christian landscape today. Catholics themselves often refer to their church simply as *The* Church. Non-Catholic Christians sometimes find this self-designation annoying, but it reflects the power and prominence that the Roman Catholic Church has historically exercised within the Christian tradition as a whole.

The word "catholic" means universal or all-encompassing, and more than any other Christian tradition, that is what Catholicism tries to be: a church where every person and every valid Christian emphasis has a place. The Catholic tradition includes an incredibly wide range of ideas, practices, attitudes, and affectivities. Rather than forcing people to choose between one style of faith or another, Catholicism has adopted a "both/and" approach where almost anything that has spiritual worth or merit can be incorporated even if the opposite emphasis is also part of the tradition. Accordingly, both celibacy and marriage are honored, retreat from the world (monasticism) and service to the world (social action) are both encouraged, and scientific inquiry is valued alongside naïve, childlike faith.

No other Christian tradition is as broad and embracing as Catholicism, but neither is any other Christian tradition so thoroughly institutional and hierarchical. Almost everything has to be approved by someone, and following the rules matters. It used to be said that Catholics had only three obligations: to pray, pay, and obey. This is no longer true. Contemporary Catholicism gives laypeople more opportunities for choice and initiative than ever before, but the tradition remains bureaucratized and stodgy. Nothing moves quickly. Even when the pope wants to change something, it often takes years of plodding effort to make it happen. The glacial pace of change can sometimes be frustrating, but Catholicism's institutional unwieldiness is one of the main reasons that the tradition can be so broad. Diversity can be tolerated because Catholicism's institutional inertia ensures that the tradition will never drift too quickly in any one direction or another.

What Is Christianity? First Edition. Douglas Jacobsen.
© 2022 John Wiley & Sons Ltd. Published 2022 by John Wiley & Sons Ltd.

Catholic Spirituality

Despite Catholicism's penchant for orderliness and control, Catholic spirituality is rooted in the unpredictable, serendipitous presence of God in the world. Catholics assume that God can appear anywhere at any time through any person, object, or event, calling people to a higher and holier way of life. The twelfth-century nun Hildegard of Bingen exuberantly described how God communicates to the world: "I gleam in the waters, and I burn in the sun, moon, and stars. With every breeze...I awaken everything to life."[1] Later, the nineteenth-century Catholic poet Gerard Manley Hopkins exulted that the whole world is "charged with the grandeur of God," ready at any moment to "flame out, like shining from shook foil."[2] Unpredictable encounters with God invite people to seize life more fully, to become better people than they already are, and to be more closely in touch with God, with others, and even with themselves.

These kinds of experiences are possible because God desires fellowship with humankind. The very first paragraph of the *Catechism of the Catholic Church* says that "God draws close" to individuals in order to encourage them "to seek him, to know him, and to love him."[3] Augustine, the ancient Bishop of Hippo in northern Africa (354–430) and the premier Catholic theologian of all time, says that people are created by God to have a relationship with God, and they are perpetually restless until they rest in God. Resting in God is the Catholic definition of prayer, which is as much a general attitude toward life as it is a specific act of talking to God. The *Catechism* describes prayer as "a vital and personal relationship with the living and true God,"[4] and it then goes on to explain that humanity's thirst for God occurs in response to God's own thirst for fellowship. In the encounter between human beings and the divine, God always takes the first step: "Whether we realize it or not, prayer is the encounter of God's thirst with ours. God thirsts that we may thirst for him."[5]

While God's presence in the world is ubiquitous, God can also sometimes be elusive, and the key role of the Church is to be the one place where God can be found without fail. Catholics believe that the Catholic Church is the "visible organization through which [Christ] communicates truth and grace to all [people]."[6] To be an active member of a local Catholic congregation is thus spiritually indispensable. It is within the Church that a person is birthed into faith, sustained in life, and ultimately delivered to God at death. The Church also distributes the sacraments, which are special acts and rituals that uniquely communicate God's grace to individuals. There are seven sacraments in all. Baptism inaugurates a person into faith, and confirmation signals the maturation of that faith. Penance and the Eucharist are repetitive acts that sustain the life of faith and help people to grow spiritually. Anointing of the sick prepares a person for a good death, defined as the ability to face life's end without fear and with trust in God. The sacraments of marriage and holy orders represent alternative life choices (at least for men): either to marry and raise children in the Catholic faith or to become a celibate priest wholly dedicated to God and the service of others. (Becoming a monk or a nun is obviously a third life choice, but this third option is not a sacrament.)

In addition to the sacraments themselves, the Catholic tradition includes a wide variety of *sacramentals* that also convey grace. These include making the sign of the cross, being sprinkled with holy water, praying the rosary, and having one's forehead marked with ashes at the beginning of Lent. Religious paintings or sculptures of Jesus, Mary, and the saints can also be sacramentals, and popular Catholic piety often focuses on these objects, which can be purchased at many Catholic churches and shrines around the world (see Figure 3.1) Sacramentals do not have the same spiritual power as the sacraments themselves, but they are in some ways more distinctively Catholic than the sacraments. Other kinds of Christians besides Catholics are baptized and celebrate the Eucharist, and they also confess their sins and sometimes do penance, but non-Catholics rarely make use of Catholic sacramentals.

Catholics believe that human beings are intimately connected to each other. Everyone's actions affect everyone else. Expressed in the negative, Catherine of Sienna (1347–1380) said: "There is no sin that does not touch others, whether secretly by refusing them what is due, or openly by giving birth to the vices."[7] The positive corollary is also true: good deeds help others and

Figure 3.1 Statues of the Infant of Prague (the young Jesus) for sale at a shop near the Church of Our Lady Victorious in Prague (Czech Republic), where the original statue is on display.

encourage the development of virtues. Ultimately, the accumulated moral choices of all the individuals in a given society slowly creates an ethos that has the power to shape and influence the morality of everyone in that society. People who grow up in selfish, materialistic cultures are more likely to become selfish and materialistic themselves in comparison to people who grow up in cultures or communities that are less selfish and more compassionate. This vision of human interconnectedness propels Catholic spirituality toward public and political engagement, including a responsibility to try nudging (or sometimes shoving) local and national laws into closer alignment with Catholic moral values.

In recent years, abortion and social justice have been especially prominent moral concerns of the Catholic Church. Pope John Paul II (in office from 1978 to 2005) described abortion as symptomatic of an increasingly toxic "culture of death" in Western society generally, and he championed what he saw as an alternative pro-life vision of sexuality, law, and cultural values. Pope Francis, who took office in 2013, has focused more on social justice and on concern for the poor and marginalized. His first encyclical, *Evangelii Gaudium*, highlighted these themes:

> We...have to say "thou shalt not" to an economy of exclusion and inequality. Such an economy kills. How can it be that it is not a news item when an elderly homeless person dies of exposure, but it is news when the stock market loses two points?...In this context, some people continue to defend trickle-down theories which assume that economic growth...will inevitably succeed in bringing about greater justice and inclusiveness in the world. This opinion, which has never been confirmed by the facts, expresses a crude and naïve trust in the goodness of those wielding economic power...Meanwhile, the excluded are still waiting.[8]

While commentators sometimes accused these two popes of being too overtly political in their views, that is a distorted view. For both popes, the intention has been to model what Catholic spirituality requires of all faithful Catholics: to pay careful attention to the deep moral values and trajectories that exist within public life and then try to influence those social standards to make them simultaneously more Catholic and more life supporting for everyone. Does this dimension of Catholic spirituality have political implications? Unquestionably, yes. Can this dimension of Catholic spirituality be reduced to mere politics? Absolutely not. Catholic morality is inherently public and it sometimes takes sides, but that is not the same as being politically partisan.

Catholicism's emphasis on humanity's interconnectedness is not limited to this world alone. Even after they die, Christians who lived exemplary lives on earth can continue to assist others from heaven as saints. Sharing God's love for people, and also fully attuned to the joys, sorrows, and temptations of human-kind, saints implore God to aid those in need, and Catholics believe they some-times intervene directly to help those who cry out for assistance. Based on their earthly lives, different saints are poised to respond more readily to certain prob-lems and desires, and Catholics call on different saints to help them in different circumstances. Saints can also become friends of a sort, and many Catholics have a favorite saint who guides them in their spiritual walk. The Catholic Church has a formal four-step process for bestowing official sainthood on indi-viduals. First, a candidate is declared to be a "Servant of God," then that person receives the status of "Venerable," next they are beatified, and finally they are canonized as a saint. Not everyone who is identified as a possible saint makes it through the whole process. While this is the formal pathway to sainthood, Catholic laypeople in various parts of the world have often treated local holy persons as saints long before they receive Church approval and sometimes in spite of the Church's formal disapproval.

The Catholic Church decided long ago that spiritual life is not restricted to religious acts and moral concerns alone; it also includes the intellect. If the entirety of the universe is God's creation, then trying to understand the uni-verse is part of Catholicism's calling. The Catholic intellectual challenge was initially described by Augustine of Hippo around the year 400 as *faith seeking understanding*, and this notion was mainstreamed into Catholic spirituality during the medieval period when Catholics built the world's first universities. The Parisian professor Thomas Aquinas (1225–1274) went so far as to argue that one of Christianity's great challenges was to take mere belief and transform it into genuine knowledge through the addition of reason. The Catholic intel-lectual tradition has flourished ever since, because Catholics assume that reli-gious faith (properly understood) and human learning (at its best) should always be mutually enlightening.

Faith has not always been properly understood, however, and learning has not always been at its best, and tensions have sometimes resulted. Infamously, the Catholic Church condemned Galileo in 1616 for suggesting that the world was part of a sun-centered rather than earth-centered system, and it took more than two centuries for the Church to reverse itself. The Catholic Church came close to making a similar mistake in the mid-nineteenth century when Charles Darwin published his famous *Origin of Species* (1859), but this time it behaved more cautiously, and in 1950 it declared that evolution, within certain limits, is compatible with Catholic teaching. Cardinal John Henry Newman (1801–1890) played a pivotal role in changing Catholic attitudes, encouraging Catholics to support academic research even when that research makes some Catholic lead-ers uneasy. Newman was convinced that ultimately scientific truth and Christian faith will bend toward each other "because truth never can really be contrary to truth."[9]

The Catholic Understanding of Salvation

Salvation in the Catholic tradition is set within a grand narrative of God's eternal love for the world and everyone in it. God made the world out of an overflowing abundance of love, and God created people to enjoy both creation and the Creator. This initial state of affairs was disrupted by sin, which is described metaphorically in the Bible's story of the Fall of Adam and Eve, and the result was devastating. Humanity was separated from God and thrown into perpetual conflict with others and with the rest of the creation. This sense of separation from God and others is called *original sin*, and Catholics believe that everyone inherits original sin at birth. (The only exception to this rule is Mary, the mother of Jesus, whom Catholics believe was conceived "immaculately" and was thus free from the curse of original sin.) Salvation is the process of undoing the effects of the Fall and restoring humanity's potential for fellowship with God. The ultimate goal of salvation is to move ever deeper into a loving relationship with God and others, recovering all that was lost in the Fall.

God's love for humanity is the backdrop for Catholicism's understanding of salvation, but for many Catholics the more immediate question concerns sin, because sin can keep people out of heaven and send them to hell. The problem of original sin is addressed by baptism, which restores one's relationship with God and washes away the guilt from all prior *sins* (individual acts of the will that transgress God's rules). But most people continue to commit at least some sins after baptism, and these need to be dealt with differently. Forgiveness for these kinds of post-baptismal sins is received through the sacrament of penance, which involves confessing one's sins to a priest, being forgiven by a priest in God's name, making restitution if possible, and then trying to avoid that sin in the future. The Catholic tradition distinguishes between *mortal sins*, serious sins like murder, theft, or adultery, and *venial sins*, like telling a white lie, that are relatively minor. Unforgiven mortal sins can send a person to hell; unforgiven venial sins will not.

Original sin can be obliterated and specific sins can be forgiven only because of the sacrificial death of Christ. This act of atonement, whereby Christ restored humanity's relationship with God, was explained by the medieval theologian Thomas Aquinas in terms of divine offense and compensation: "By suffering out of love and obedience, Christ gave more to God than was required to compensate for the offense of the whole human race. ...And therefore, Christ's Passion was not only a sufficient but a superabundant atonement for the sins of the human race."[10] Aquinas, like all Catholic theologians, emphasizes that it is Christ's *voluntary* self-sacrifice that makes the difference. On the cross, Christ freely absorbed all of the punishment that humanity rightly deserves for its sins, and this explains why the crucifix is such an important object in the Catholic tradition. The crucifix portrays the key act in the drama of salvation, Christ's willing embrace of pain and death in order to secure humanity's redemption.

The true goal of salvation is not, however, merely the forgiveness of sins; it is the full restoration of fellowship between God and humankind. This divine relationship-building involves a lengthy process that Catholics call "conversion of the heart" (or simply conversion), and it has some similarities to the process of *theosis* or deification in the Orthodox tradition. Full conversion of the heart is the result of a lifetime of worship, obedience, confession, reconciliation, service, and prayer. Some Catholics dedicate themselves entirely to this work by taking religious vows and becoming religious brothers or sisters (monks or nuns). Other Catholics seek conversion of their hearts while remaining "in the world," trying as best they can to live in God's presence and do God's will while also fulfilling their other responsibilities as family members, workers, neighbors, friends, and citizens.

The most important spiritual aid to conversion offered by the Catholic Church is the Eucharist. The word "Eucharist" itself means thanksgiving, and the Eucharistic celebration is a way to participate in and give thanks for Christ's sacrifice on the cross. Catholics believe that the Eucharistic bread and wine literally become the body and blood of Christ, a process called transubstantiation, and that ingesting the body and blood of Christ feeds them spiritually. In the words of Julian of Norwich (1342–1416): "Our precious Mother Jesus can feed us with himself, and does, most courteously and most tenderly, with the blessed sacrament, which is the precious food of true life."[11] Mother Teresa, the twentieth-century humanitarian saint from Calcutta, said that the Eucharist was her spiritual food and that she could not survive a single day without it. Simply being in the presence of the consecrated host (the bread) can convey grace, and most Catholic churches display a consecrated host somewhere inside the building (in a room or location called an adoration chapel) so that people can kneel, pray, and meditate in Christ's presence.

The Catholic tradition has wrestled with the question of whether salvation is available in any form outside the institution of the Roman Catholic Church. Historically, the answer has been "no," but some Catholic theologians now suggest that individuals can be "anonymous Christians" outside the Catholic Church who can reach heaven through their unconscious desire for baptism. The Catholic Catechism seems to affirm this possibility of salvation outside the church when it states that while "God has bound salvation to the sacrament of baptism...he himself is not bound by his sacraments."[12] Nonetheless, almost all Catholics would say that the only truly safe and assured pathway to salvation runs through the Catholic Church.

Until recently, Catholics, like most other Christians, thought about salvation almost entirely in terms of life after death. Now it is commonly argued that salvation can and should also be experienced to some degree in this life. Catholic liberation theologians say this quest for earthly salvation applies specially to the poor, who currently live undeservedly in an earthly hell of poverty and oppression. Some Catholic feminist theologians apply the same principle to women and often to anyone who is marginalized or oppressed. These present-focused Catholics do not agree that salvation is only or mostly a future event; salvation must manifest itself in some way in the here and now.

The ultimate purpose of salvation is holiness, sufficient holiness to enter heaven and stand in God's presence without shame or embarrassment. Since most humans do not achieve this level of holiness while still living on earth, Catholicism has developed the idea of purgatory, a postmortem spiritual experience that allows individuals to complete their journey toward holiness after death. There are only a few references to something like purgatory in the Bible (see, for example, Matthew 5:25–26, I Corinthians 3:12–13, and II Maccabees 12:42–46), but the idea of purgatory is a necessary conclusion given the Catholic logic of salvation. If real and actual holiness is a prerequisite for fellowship with God, then God will provide some pathway for human beings to achieve that holiness because God loves people and genuinely wants their fellowship.

Catholic History

The Catholic tradition claims roots that go back to Jesus himself and to Peter, his apostle, to whom Christ gave "the keys of the kingdom of heaven" (Matthew 16:19). Catholics view Peter as the first bishop of Rome (the first pope) and as the founder of the Catholic Church. The papacy as it exists today was created much later, and the Catholic tradition itself did not coalesce into anything like what it is now until the eleventh and twelfth centuries, but the deep roots of Catholicism can be traced back to the ancient Roman Empire and the Roman Imperial Church. More specifically, Catholic Christianity descended from the Latin-speaking half of the Roman Imperial Church, and it was originally part of the larger Chalcedonian movement that emerged out of the Great Division. During the 600 years following that division, the Catholic Church slowly developed its own theological and ecclesiastical identity that differed from Eastern Orthodoxy, its former Chalcedonian partner.

Many of the differences that emerged between nascent Catholicism and Eastern Orthodoxy sprang from larger social developments over which neither Catholics nor Orthodox Christians had any control. The most significant change was the demise of the western Roman Empire. The city of Rome was sacked by the Visigoths in 410, and by 450 the entire western half of the empire had been conquered and partitioned into several smaller states controlled by different Germanic tribes. The Western Roman Church had to maneuver to keep itself alive in this newly complex political environment. The Bishop of Rome quickly stepped into the role of keeping the Church united, which remains a key objective of the papal office today, and the Church developed a new understanding of itself as an international body of believers in Christ rather than as the church of one specific empire. Augustine of Hippo, the great bishop from North Africa, saw the implications almost immediately, and he described the Western Church as "catholic" (meaning universal) rather than imperial. In contrast to Orthodoxy's ethnic connections, Catholicism defines itself as "a society of pilgrims of all languages, not scrupling about diversities in the[ir] manners, laws, and institutions."[13]

The Conversion of Europe, 500 to 1000

Following the collapse of the western Roman Empire, Christians found themselves surrounded by people who were either not Christians or not the right kinds of Christians. Many of the invading people groups were religiously pagan; others were Arian Christians, following the teachings of Arius of Alexandria who promoted the view that Christ was less than fully divine. In all cases, the papally-led Church felt duty bound to convert them. The Franks were the first to embrace Catholic Christianity around the year 500. Spain and England followed a hundred years later. Germany joined the Catholic ranks shortly thereafter, and finally Scandinavia submitted to Catholic Christianity, around the year 1000.

Conversion is never a simple process. It affects both the converted and the converters, and the conversion of Western Europe deeply influenced the emerging Catholic tradition. Spain provides an interesting illustration. Following the collapse of the western Roman Empire, Spain was colonized by the Visigoths who were Arian Christians. When they converted to Catholic Christianity in the late 590s, they felt compelled to distance themselves from their heretical past by hyper-emphasizing Christ's equality with God the Creator. As one means of doing so, they added the word *filioque* to the Nicaean Creed which they recited in worship. *Filioque* means "and the son," and this word was inserted after the word "Father" in the creed's clause about the Holy Spirit. Rather than proceeding from the Father alone, the Holy Spirit was now said to proceed from the Father *and the Son*. This addition changed the implied relationship between the persons of the Trinity, giving Christ higher status than the Holy Spirit, and within just a few centuries this became the standard wording in the creed used by all Christians in Western Europe. This change, which was made unilaterally in the West, deeply offended Orthodox Christians who saw it not only as theologically invalid, but also as a breach of Christian etiquette. In their view, the Nicaean Creed, which had originally been approved by a council that included Christians from both the West and the East, could be modified only if both sides agreed with the change. In this case the East had not been consulted, and it did not approve.

Western, Catholic Christianity was also altered as a consequence of converting the German tribes of northern Europe. One example is the use of the word "Easter" as a name for Christianity's holiest holiday. The term Easter is derived

from the name of a Northern European pagan goddess "Eostre" who was associated with dawn, the spring planting season, and fertility in general. Using this
word for the holiday connected the notion of newness or rebirth to the Christian
ideas of resurrection and salvation, helping a newly converted population to
better understand the concepts and values of Christianity. However, using this
name also changed the day's religious emphasis. In the East (and in southern
Europe), the same holy day is called "Pascha," a reference to the Jewish Passover
with which it coincides. Pascha highlights the historical context of Christ's
death and resurrection, while the term Easter underscores God's timeless
promise of redemption and new life. The difference in emphasis is subtle, but it
foreshadows Catholicism's emerging self-identity as the custodian of timeless
truth in contrast to Eastern Orthodoxy's emphasis on the importance of time
and place. None of these local, cultural adaptations of Christianity in the West
prompted a formal break with the Orthodox Christianity of the East, but each
contributed a bit more tension to the relationship.

Consolidating the Catholic Tradition, 1000 to 1500

Shortly after the year 1000 – that is, shortly after Western Europe had been fully
converted to Christianity – the Catholic Church decisively split with Eastern
Orthodoxy. The breakpoint came in the year 1054 when leaders of the two
churches reciprocally condemned each other, which cleared the way for the
Catholic Church to launch a massive effort to consolidate itself institutionally
and to codify its increasingly non-Eastern Orthodox practices and beliefs.

This new consolidation of the Catholic Church was initiated by Pope Gregory
VII, who held office from 1073 to 1085. Pope Gregory wanted to establish tighter
control over the Catholic Church as a whole, but at the time he took office it
was still common for local political rulers to oversee the selection and appointment of bishops in their jurisdictions. This made sense given that many of these
locally appointed bishops were wealthy landowners who possessed not only
religious authority but also significant political clout. Pope Gregory wanted to
make it clear, however, that bishops were first and foremost religious leaders
whose primary loyalty should be to the Church. Predictably, the Pope and the
German emperor (who was the most powerful political ruler in the region and
had the title "Holy Roman Emperor") were soon engaged in a prolonged dispute known as the Investiture Controversy to determine which of them got to
select and *invest* bishops with the power and symbols of their office. Over time,
Pope Gregory and his successors slowly solidified their right to select most bishops, and this power of appointment enabled the popes to advance other reforms
within the Church.

In the twelfth century, the Catholic Church commenced a frenzy of activity
seeking to improve the clergy and clarify the core teachings of the Church. Nine

general councils were held between the years 1123 and 1445 – there have only been twenty-one general councils in all Catholic history – and these nine councils largely defined the Catholic tradition as it still exists today. Key theological ideas like transubstantiation, purgatory, the immaculate conception of Mary, and the seven sacraments were formalized; new institutional structures like the Roman Curia and the College of Cardinals were created; and new professional standards for the priesthood were enunciated. This is when celibacy became mandatory for priests and when priests were first required to wear distinctive clothing in public.

The Catholic worldview that emerged during these years emphasized the regularity and predictability of the world as God had created it and the orderliness of salvation, as well. The Catholic Church was portrayed as God's primary (or only) vehicle for funneling grace into the world, and it was the Church's role to dispense the means of salvation properly. Catholicism's emphasis on orderliness and reason was architecturally displayed in the great Gothic cathedrals of the era, which even today impress visitors with their symmetry and serenity. Rationality and predictability were also central to the rise of the Catholic university system, where scholastic theologians devoted themselves to proving the reasonableness of every Catholic practice and belief.

The religious self-confidence that permeated medieval Catholicism was undoubtedly reassuring to ordinary Catholic believers, but it could be frightening and dangerous for people who were not Catholic. During these centuries, heretics (Christians who held views that differed from the official teachings of the Church) were condemned and persecuted as part of the Catholic Inquisition, Jews were expelled from many Christian territories, and Orthodox Christians were frequently described as spiritually defective. Muslims were declared to be enemies of God, and the Church supported a series of military expeditions to the Middle East (called "Crusades") that were intended to defeat Islam and to reclaim the Holy Land for Christ.

At the very same time that many Catholic Church leaders were trying to maximize both their own power and the social power of the Church, other Catholic visionaries were emphasizing precisely the opposite ideal: the need to be humble and to love and serve others. Francis of Assisi epitomized this alternative. The son of a wealthy Italian merchant, young Francis had a vision of Jesus – a crucifix in the Church of San Damiano in Assisi spoke to him – and he was transformed. He gave up his riches and devoted himself to Lady Poverty, determined to treat the persons and bodies of others, especially the sick and poor, as he would have treated Christ himself. He even wandered to Egypt where he tried unsuccessfully to end the Crusades by peaceably converting the Sultan who led the anti-Crusader Muslim army. If one emotion dominated Francis's life it was joy in the presence of God, and his attitude was infectious. He soon developed a loyal following, which he organized into the Franciscan religious order. And Francis was not alone. Many other Catholics of the period, including his friend Clare (who started a parallel Franciscan order for women called the

Poor Clares), dedicated themselves to these same ideals, and concern for the poor has been an integral component of the Catholic tradition ever since.

Catholicism Challenged and Reaffirmed: 1500 to 1900

The sixteenth century was a tumultuous time for the Catholic tradition. Even before 1500, Catholics had begun spreading the Christian message to Africa, Asia, and the Americas, and Catholicism would soon become the most widely dispersed religion on earth. But in Europe, the Catholic Church was being challenged as never before. Most notably, a religious revolt called Protestantism had arisen in northern Germany and was quickly spreading into England, Switzerland, the Low Countries, and Scandinavia, and even temporarily into France and Poland. Protestantism would eventually lure about 20 percent of the European population away from the Catholic Church.

The Council of Trent, which met intermittently from 1545 to 1563, was both a response to Protestantism and a reaffirmation of Catholic self-confidence. The Council acknowledged a handful of abuses that needed to be addressed, but the focus of the meeting was on criticizing Protestant errors and reaffirming Catholic thought and practice as it had been codified during the previous 500 years. Education was a central concern, because laypeople and even priests were often unfamiliar with the official teachings of the Church. Bishops were charged with correcting this deficiency, and much of the legwork fell to the newly formed Society of Jesus (the Jesuits) which founded hundreds of new schools across Europe. The Jesuits were also indispensable to the work of global Catholic missions, helping to translate the gospel into concepts and languages that were accessible to the non-Christian populations and cultures of Africa, Asia, and the Americas.

The Catholic Church, and the Jesuits in particular, were aware that faith is not a matter of belief and moral practice alone; it is also an affective orientation to God, others, and the world. Understanding this, a new style of church architecture was developed with the goal of promoting proper Catholic affections. Earlier medieval Gothic cathedrals were designed to reflect the rationality and orderliness of faith. The new Baroque churches of the late sixteenth and seventeenth centuries were, by contrast, designed to overwhelm worshipers with their frantic beauty. Every space in a Baroque church is alive with movement, energy, and celebration (see Figure 3.2). The goal is for worshipers to experience a foretaste of the glories of heaven. Baroque architecture is an expression of Catholicism at its grandest, and its exuberance was meant to differentiate Catholicism from the boring plainness of Protestantism and its undecorated churches.

The optimism of the Baroque period held sway for nearly two centuries before a new challenge arose. It emanated from France, and it was partly intellectual in character and partly institutional. Eighteenth-century *philosophes* (public intellectuals) like Voltaire (1694–1778) asserted that the Catholic Church was

Figure 3.2 Chiesa di Sant'Ignazio di Loyola, a Baroque style Catholic church in Rome built in the early 1600s, showing apse at the front of the sanctuary and details from the painted ceiling.

both repressive and immoral. Voltaire was so disgusted with the Church that he signed all his personal correspondence with the phrase "écrasez l'infâme," which means "crush the loathsome thing." Crushing the Catholic Church turned into actual policy during the French Revolution (1789–1799) when Catholicism was banned from France and a new religion of reason was established in its place. Radical ideas from France soon spread elsewhere, and the Catholic Church felt under siege. After the Revolution was over, European political leaders met at the Congress of Vienna (1814–1815) hoping to restore the old conservative order of Europe, but it ultimately proved impossible to resurrect the pre-revolutionary hierarchical social order.

Political developments and Catholic social ideals continued to diverge during the nineteenth century, and the Catholic Church became increasingly reactionary. This is evident in the pontificate of Pius IX, the longest serving of all Catholic popes (in office from 1846 to 1878). In 1864, Pope Pius IX issued a *Syllabus of Errors* denouncing everything modern, including freedom of the press, public schools, and democracy. As the Catholic Church distanced itself from democratic (in contrast to monarchical) politics, it simultaneously gave more attention to explicitly spiritual matters, and the end result was that the spiritual authority of the papacy increased as the pope's political influence decreased. This trend culminated in the proclamation of the doctrine of papal infallibility in 1870.

As the pope gained new power at the top of the Church structure, laypeople were simultaneously securing new control over their own spiritual lives. Grassroots religious activism increased dramatically, especially among women. New religious orders like the Sisters of Charity (founded in 1809) and the Sisters of Mercy (founded in 1831) turned their spiritual energy toward the needs of the poor, and new saints like Thérèse of Lisieux (1873–1897) provided models of Catholic faithfulness that were accessible to everyone. Thérèse became a Carmelite nun at age fifteen and died of tuberculosis less than ten years later, but her writings changed the Catholic world. Her "little way" of faith emphasized the importance of small acts of love and kindness that anyone could perform, and she assured Catholics that God valued these small but faithful efforts as much as any grand act of leadership, devotion, or even martyrdom.

> [God] showed me...that every flower created by Him is beautiful, that the brilliance of the rose and the whiteness of the lily do not lessen the perfume of the violet or the sweet simplicity of the daisy. I understood that if all the lowly flowers wished to be roses, nature would lose its springtide beauty, and the fields would no longer be enameled with lovely hues. And so it is in the world of souls, Our Lord's living garden. He has been pleased to create great Saints who may be compared to the lily and the rose, but He has also created lesser ones, who must be content to be daisies or simple violets flowering at His Feet, and whose mission it is to gladden His Divine Eyes when He deigns to look down on them.[14]

Uncharted Territory: 1900 to the Present

The twentieth century was a time of unprecedented progress and of equally unprecedented challenges for humankind. Catholicism, like all other Christian traditions, struggled to adapt to these changes, and the Second Vatican Council (1962–1965) was an especially important pivot point. Pope John XXIII, who convened the council, said its main purpose was *aggiornamento*, a radical updating of the Church to make it more responsive to the spiritual needs of the modern world. This sentiment is epitomized in the opening lines of the council's most famous declaration *Gaudium et Spes*, which explicitly linked the Church's role in the world to the flourishing of humanity in general:

> The joys and the hopes, the griefs and the anxieties of the [people] of this age, especially those who are poor or in any way afflicted, these are the joys and hopes, the griefs and anxieties of the followers of Christ. Indeed, nothing genuinely human fails to raise an echo in their hearts.[15]

Enthusiasm ran high after the council, but the task of interpreting and implementing its conclusions was more complicated than expected. Subsequent popes were more cautious than Pope John XXIII, and it was hard to address all of the joys, hopes, griefs, and anxieties of the world when neither Catholics nor people in general agreed on what those joys, hopes, griefs, and anxieties were. Vatican II itself eventually became a bone of contention, with Catholic progressives and Catholic conservatives nurturing very different interpretations of its meaning and significance.

Despite these difficulties, Catholicism has flourished as a global religion. There were roughly a quarter of a billion Catholics in the world in 1900, and there are five times that number today. Catholics now live literally everywhere. In 1900, two-thirds of all Catholics still resided in Europe; today three-quarters live outside of Europe, with the single largest contingent (40 percent of all Catholics) located in Latin America. The Catholic tradition has become multi-cultural, and the addition of new voices from Africa, Asia, Latin America, and North America have enriched and challenged Catholicism's historically Eurocentric way of seeing the world. Latin American Catholics often call for greater emphasis on social justice, Africans champion the role of the family, Asians ask for more accommodation of non-Christian religious values, and North Americans want the Church to become more democratic. It is a raucous conversation, but it also signals the Church's overall health. There is, however, one problem that hovers over the Catholic Church and threatens its future: the sexual abuse crisis that has involved so many children, so many priests, and so many Church leaders who looked the other way for decades. Unless and until the Catholic Church can rebuild the trust that has been lost, its future remains in limbo.

Institutional and Social Structure of Catholicism

Catholicism differs institutionally from the other three major Christian tradi-tions because it is housed in one united organization and has one indisputable leader. That leader has numerous titles including Bishop of Rome, Vicar of Christ, Supreme Pontiff of the Universal Church, and Servant of the Servants of God, but the term "pope" is most common. Pope simply means "papa," and the Catholic pope is the papa of Catholicism, the kindly and wise leader of the Catholic family of faith. Theologically, the central role of the papacy is to serve as a symbol of unity, to be "the perpetual and visible source of the unity both of the bishops and of the whole company of the faithful."[16] The pope is also uniquely vested with the task of proclaiming the faith and interpreting its meaning. This role is often linked in people's minds to the doctrine of papal infallibility, and they assume that everything the pope says is binding on all Catholics. But papal infallibility only applies when the pope explicitly declares himself to be speaking *ex cathedra*. The doctrine of papal infallibility, promul-gated by the First Vatican Council in 1870, has only been invoked once, in 1950, when the assumption of Mary (the bodily taking up of Mary into heaven at the time of her death) was declared to be a required article of faith for all Catholics.

While the pope's main role is spiritual, he also oversees a huge organization. In fact, the Roman Catholic Church is the largest non-governmental organiza-tion in the world. It has a global membership of roughly 1.3 billion people and is served by about 5500 bishops and 400,000 priests. The Catholic Church owns and operates 125,000 schools worldwide, including approximately 200 universities, and it runs more than 100,000 other charitable institutions, including hospitals, orphanages, and homes for the elderly and the needy. Additionally, the pope rules his own nation, the Vatican, which is the smallest country in the world. It does, however, have its own army, the Swiss Guard (135 soldiers who wear distinctive ceremonial uniforms striped in red, yellow, and blue), and it carries on diplomatic relations with other nations through its Secretary of State.

The administrative tasks of the Catholic Church are handled through the Roman Curia, which consists of a variety of different offices that monitor and govern Catholic life around the world. The Curia includes nine important subunits, called "congregations," that focus on different areas of church life such as doctrine, worship, education, evangelism, and the clergy. The Curia also includes a vast array of councils and agencies that deal with everything from interreligious dialogue and the pastoral care of immigrants to running the Vatican Library and keeping track of Catholic Church statistics. All these offices are crammed mazelike into the Vatican's 110 acres, and maneuvering through this maze can be confusing, both literally and institutionally. Given the size of the job and the leanness of staff, however, the Curia works surprisingly well, even if it can sometimes be slow, cumbersome, and complicated.

Very few Catholics ever interact personally with the pope or the Roman Curia. The Catholic Church that most people know is the Church that is supervised by its bishops. On this level, the Church is divided into more than 3000 geographical districts. Most of these units are called dioceses, though some have other names like eparchy, vicariate, or prefecture. A bishop or archbishop oversees every diocese, and the bishop (or more typically the archbishop) of the oldest or most important diocese in a nation is sometimes called the primate of that country. The pope appoints the bishops, who serve for life, and they have total responsibility for the Catholic Church within their dioceses. It is difficult to remove a bishop from office, with exceptions only for grave acts of sin or misconduct. In the past, bishops often vigorously guarded their independence, but over the last half century they have slowly become more collegial, forming themselves into various national and regional councils of bishops that share ideas and coordinate actions. The Council of Latin American Bishops (*Consejo Episcopal Latinoamericano* or CELAM), for example, was instrumental in developing and promoting many of the ideas that later found systematic expression in liberation theology, and more recently the Federation of Asian Bishops' Conferences (FABC) has helped direct attention both to issues of poverty and to interreligious dialogue.

Catholic dioceses are sub-divided into parishes, and the local parish is the heart of religious life for most Catholics. It is in the face-to-face context of the local parish that Catholicism becomes a living faith expressed in community with everyone else who is a member of that parish. Normally there is only one church building per parish, with one or more priests assigned to care for the spiritual needs of the local Catholic population. Catholics living within the bounds of a given parish are expected to attend the church in that parish, but Catholics who live in urban or suburban settings with several nearby parishes will occasionally shop around to find the specific parish they like best.

In much of the Catholic world priests are in short supply, and parishes are underserved because of it. This is especially the case in Latin America where the shortage of Catholic priests is one of the reasons Catholics are converting to Pentecostalism. The shortage of priests has led some Catholics to suggest that married men and perhaps even women should be able to become priests, but so far these suggestions have been vigorously rejected by the Catholic Church hierarchy. In the meanwhile, many parishes now hire lay ecclesiastical ministers to help priests do their work, and many of these ministers are women. Priests are also being assisted by *permanent* deacons, a position first created in the 1960s. (This is a different role than being a *transitional* deacon, which is a step on the way to the priesthood.) Permanent deacons, many of whom are married, can perform more tasks than lay ecclesiastical ministers, but one exception is the Eucharist, which can only be consecrated by a priest. There are currently about 35,000 permanent deacons worldwide, and their numbers are growing.

In addition to its diocesan structure, the Catholic Church includes a separate organizational structure for individuals who have chosen to live a "consecrated life" wholly set apart for God. These individuals are known as "the religious," and the generic name for the organizations to which they belong is "religious institute." Most Catholic brothers are not priests, but sometimes they are; the Society of Jesus (the Jesuits), in particular, requires all members to be ordained clergy. Historically, the consecrated life stretches back to the first century, when certain widows took on special roles of service and devotion within the early Christian community. The consecrated life took new shape around the year 300 when people like Anthony the Great (251–356) left the civilized world behind and headed into the Egyptian desert to be alone with God. These individuals were called monks, which comes from the Greek word *monos*, meaning "one" or "alone." Eventually, most monks and nuns joined communities where they could look after each other, usually under the guidance of an elder (an abbot or abbess) who was simultaneously a teacher, spiritual exemplar, and enforcer of rules. Some groups of brothers or sisters remain cloistered today and only rarely have any contact with the outside world, but this is now rare. Most consecrated Catholics today are engaged in social service or some other form of service within the Church that requires interaction with people outside their own monastic community.

Throughout the centuries, but especially in recent decades, Catholic laypeople have also developed a variety of organizations for serving others and the

Church and for fostering their own spiritual development. In the past, these kinds of organizations (often called "confraternities") were frequently dedicated to a specific saint or to some approved devotional practice. Today, these organizations, now called *new ecclesiastical movements* (NEM), typically address some social need. Focolare, one of most well-known NEMs, founded by Chiara Lubich in Italy in 1943, seeks to encourage human unity at all levels – interpersonally, locally, nationally, and globally. The president of Focolare must be a Catholic laywoman, and a priest always serves as co-president. The organization currently has about 150,000 members subdivided into twenty-two geographic regions around the world. There are hundreds of other NEMs around the globe that vary enormously in terms of purpose, size, organizational structure, and membership expectations, and together these groups are encouraging an unprecedented level of social and spiritual activity within the Catholic laity.

There is abundant diversity in Catholicism, but Catholics worldwide remain bound together by their shared faith and religious practice, and most notably by the Mass. Wherever in the world the Mass is celebrated, whoever is involved, and whatever language is being used, Catholics know they are home when Mass begins. Participation in the Mass feels a bit like slipping into a comfortable old pair of shoes. Everyone knows what to do, and they do it together, and it is that sense of spiritual oneness that holds the Catholic community together. No one expects all Catholics to look, think, or act alike, but everyone expects that Mass will draw them together. This is the genius of Catholicism: The Church provides a shared framework of faith, but each person's walk with God is presumed to be unique. Catholics may think of their church as *The* Church, but it is not monolithic. The Church allows Catholics to practice their shared faith in a myriad of ways, and it is this combination of community and freedom that continues to keep more than half the world's Christians firmly Catholic.

Notes

1 Matthew Fox, ed., *Hildegard of Bingen's Book of Divine Works with Letters and Songs* (Santa Fe, NM: Bear and Company, 1987), pp. 8–10.

2 Gerard Manley Hopkins, *Poems of Gerard Manley Hopkins*, 3rd edition (New York: Oxford University Press, 1948), p. 70.

3 *Catechism of the Catholic Church*, paragraph 1.

4 *Catechism*, paragraph 2558.

5 *Catechism*, paragraph 2560.

6 *Catechism*, paragraph 771.

7 Catherine of Sienna, *The Dialogue*, translated by Suzanne Noffke (New York: Paulist Press, 1980), p. 35.

8 Pope Francis, *Evancelii Gaudium*, paragraph 11

9 John Henry Newman, *The Idea of a University* (New Haven, CT: Yale University Press, 1996), p. 230.

10 Thomas Aquinas, *Summa Theologica* III:48.2.

11 *Julian of Norwich: Showings*, translated by Edmund College and James Walsh (New York: Paulist, 1978), p. 298.

12 *Catechism*, paragraph 1257.

13 Augustine, *The City of God*, translated by Marcus Dods (New York: Modern Library, 1993), p. 696.

14 Thérèse of Lisieux, *The Autobiography of Thérèse of Lisieux: The Story of a Soul*, translated by John Beevers (New York: Image, 2011), pp. 2–3.

15 *Gaudium et Spes*, paragraph 1.

16 *Catechism*, paragraph 882.

4

Protestantism

The Bible and the Individual

Protestantism bolted onto the scene suddenly in the sixteenth century without having time to fully vet or synchronize its message. Yet Protestantism's core proclamation was clear: Christians need to trust God, read the Bible for themselves, and rely on their own best thinking when deciding what to believe and how to act as followers of Jesus. Protestant reformers were aware that the church as an institution could help individuals in this task, but they thought it could also hinder, and the early Protestant reformers were convinced that the Catholic Church of their age was doing more harm than good. In place of a tradition that emphasized predictability and assurance, Protestantism offered an alternative view of God and humanity that de-institutionalized salvation and accentuated personal faith. In doing so, Protestantism not only gave birth to a new variety of Christianity, it also laid the foundation for the modern West's emphasis on the importance of the individual.

Protestants were (and still are) looking for a faith that is applicable to every-day life. They want to get their doctrines correct, sometimes obsessively so, but even more they want a faith that provides guidance for life in the ordinary workaday world. The famous twentieth-century Protestant theologian Karl Barth reportedly said that being a faithful Christian requires reading the Bible in one hand and the newspaper in the other. This duality of focus, studying the Bible and applying it ever anew to the current realities of human history, is what drives Protestantism forward. Protestants know that this work will never be done. Improving the world is a slow slog, and new challenges often arise before older challenges have been fully addressed. So, Protestants see faith as a quest. The goal is to be "reformed, but ever reforming." In a telling comment, the pilgrim pastor John Robinson reminded his parishioners before they set off for North America in 1620 that God had "more truth and light yet to break forth out of his holy word."[1] Protestantism is a movement in motion, and in that movement the Bible serves as both its anchor and its beacon for the future.

The founders of Protestantism considered the open-endedness of their faith to be a virtue; the Catholic Church did not. When the Protestant movement first

What Is Christianity? First Edition. Douglas Jacobsen.
© 2022 John Wiley & Sons Ltd. Published 2022 by John Wiley & Sons Ltd.

began, Catholics viewed it as spiritually restless and predicted that it would soon shatter into an array of competing groups and subgroups. Many Catholics still believe that Protestantism is inherently individualistic and tends toward religious chaos. This criticism undoubtedly exaggerates the faults of Protestantism, but it is not entirely false. As an example, one could point to Roger Williams, the Protestant founder of the colony of Rhode Island, who eventually concluded that only he, and possibly his wife, understood Christianity properly. Most Protestants do not, however, take things to that extreme. They value their spiritual freedom, but they also want at least some other Protestants to agree with them and validate their views. Thus while Protestantism can be spiritually rambunctious, most Protestants are not nearly as freewheeling as either their most radical proponents or their Catholic critics suggest.

The term "Protestant" does not convey the same kind of religious identity as Catholic or Orthodox. This is because "Protestant" is a general term, and many Protestants prefer more precise labels to describe their religious affiliation. They call themselves Baptists or Lutherans or Presbyterians or some other name, rather than referring to themselves as generic Protestants. On the other hand, some Protestants prefer to say that they are "just Christian" and resist being more specific. Protestants tend to view Catholics and Orthodox Christians as shaped by their particular church traditions, but they see themselves as simply reading the Bible and believing what it says with no need for any tradition to help them interpret the text. Hence, they think of themselves as just Christians without any special distinguishing marks. Using the term "Christian" as a synonym for Protestant has, in fact, become so prevalent that in many countries a person who claims to be "Christian" will almost automatically be understood to be saying they are Protestant (or possibly Pentecostal) in contrast to being Catholic or Orthodox.

Protestant Spirituality

It is almost impossible to overstate the Bible's importance within Protestantism. The Bible is the foundation for everything else. It is not just another book. It is *the* book, the book of books, the book that interprets all other books, and indeed the book that interprets life itself. The Rev. Billy Graham, probably the most well-known Protestant preacher of the twentieth century, never tired of punctuating his sermons with the three-word phrase "the Bible says." Graham was a conservative evangelical, but similar sentiments are expressed across the spectrum of Protestant churches. For example, pastors in the American-based United Church of Christ, one of the most progressive Protestant denominations in the world, often introduce their reflections on the Bible with the auspicious preamble: "God is still speaking."

Most Protestants assume that no special training is necessary in order to hear what God is saying through the words of the Bible. The only requirement is to read it with the intention to obey what it says. This was the German reformer Martin Luther's argument when he was hauled before the Holy Roman Emperor Charles V in 1521 and told to recant his Protestant views. Luther replied that he could not and would not change his mind unless he was "convinced by Scripture and plain reason." His basic point was simple: God speaks clearly through the Bible, and Luther was not about to disagree with God. Protestants later formalized this belief in the doctrine of scriptural *perspicacity*, the claim that the Bible's meaning will be clear to anyone who reads it with an open mind. The American Congregationalist pastor R. A. Torrey (1856–1928) rather pugnaciously explained: "The Bible is one of the easiest books in the world to understand if [people] really wish to understand it and to find out what it actually teaches, and do not wish to read into it their own notions and speculations."[2]

Protestantism has historically stressed that people have the *right* to read and interpret the Bible for themselves, and this right of private interpretation comes with a corresponding responsibility: all Christians have a *duty* to read the Bible for themselves. Reading the Bible is so central to their vision of Christian life that Protestants have labored long and hard to make the Bible available to everyone, both by translating the Bible into ever more languages and also by creating thousands of schools around the world to teach people how to read. Largely because of Protestant efforts, the Bible has now been fully translated into more than 650 languages and partially translated into 2000 more. A host of Protestant organizations and Bible societies have distributed the Bible to anyone who wants one. One of the most well-known, the Gideons, founded in 1899 by two American salesmen, has given away more than two billion copies of the Bible worldwide.

The Bible is where Protestants turn when they need spiritual recharging. Protestants read the Bible at home by themselves, they read it in small groups, and they read it together in church. They sometimes read the Bible in search of spiritual comfort; its familiar words remind them of who they are, and the act of reading itself reassures them of God's love and care. But Protestants also read the Bible to figure out what to believe and how to live, and Protestants do not always agree about what it says. This may appear to conflict with the doctrine of the Bible's perspicacity, but most Protestants are not bothered by the apparent contradiction. They believe the Bible is relatively clear, but they also know that people read it in slightly different ways. That is just the way life is.

Protestantism's different interpretations of the Bible (and the different theologies that have emerged as a result) have sometimes led to argument and debate, but the more common response has been simply to associate with people who read the Bible in a similar way. Like birds of a feather, Protestants tend to flock together with other like-minded believers. These compatible groups have names like Anglican, Baptist, Methodist, Reformed, and Lutheran, and each group reads the Bible through its own lens. These lenses or interpretive frameworks are sometimes called "canons within the canon," selected passages of scripture that seem especially clear in meaning which can then be used to clarify the meaning of other passages that seem less clear. Lutherans, for example, often cite the New Testament book of Galatians as their canon within the canon, utilizing its sharp distinction between law and grace to guide their reading of the rest of the Bible. Presbyterian and Reformed Protestants tend to prefer the book of Romans because it gives more attention to God's providential control over human history. Mennonites and other Anabaptists are attracted to Jesus's Sermon on the Mount (found in both Matthew and Luke) because of its emphasis on pacifism and practical Christian living. Many Baptists underscore the importance of one verse, John 3:16, because it communicates that a personal decision is required for salvation and they read the rest of the Bible in that light.

While Protestants read the Bible for themselves, they also look to their different churches for guidance, and the single most important person in this regard is the local pastor. Like priests in the Catholic and Orthodox traditions, Protestant pastors try to address all the different spiritual needs of their parishioners, but Protestant pastors are also expected to be biblical scholars. Most Protestant churches require their pastors to be seminary-educated, and most seminaries require students to have some familiarity with the Bible's two original languages of Hebrew and Greek. The bookshelves of Protestant ministers are typically filled with Bible commentaries, and all this learning gets funneled into the weekly sermon, which is the central event in most Protestant worship services. Protestants often refer to their pastors as preachers, because delivering the weekly sermon – preaching – is their most important function. The significance of preaching is also reflected in the architecture of many Protestant churches where the pulpit, rather than the altar or Communion table, is front and center (see Figure 4.1).

Protestant sermons are complex performances. On the one hand, they are like classroom lectures, with pastors carefully explaining the meaning of the biblical text to their students (the parishioners). On the other hand, they often resemble a form of entertainment or public debate because pastors are expected to hold the attention of their audiences and to convince everyone that their conclusions make sense. Protestant pastors cannot dictate what their parishioners must believe; they can only try to persuade them. And Protestant laypeople know this. They listen carefully to their pastors' sermons because they want to learn, but they also listen critically and reserve the right to disagree if they think their pastor has gotten something wrong. This same kind of critical loyalty applies to the entirety of the Protestant pastor's role. On the one hand, Protestant pastors are the religious leaders of the congregations they serve, but on the other hand they are employees of the congregation and in some denominations can be dismissed at will. This is a stressful tightrope to walk, and pastoral burnout is not uncommon.

Figure 4.1   Interior of Hungarian Reformed Church in Sibiu, Romania illustrating the centrality of the pulpit in Protestant church architecture.

Protestantism tends toward egalitarianism. Everybody has equal spiritual standing before God, and everyone has some role to play in the kingdom of God. The pastor's job is unique, but it is only one of many callings or vocations that Protestants may have. For Catholics and Orthodox Christians, to have a religious vocation is to become a priest or to take vows and join a consecrated religious community. This is precisely what Protestants reject. The work of the church is good and necessary, but Protestants believe that other work in the world is also good, necessary, and God-ordained. Being a good mother or father can be a Protestant vocation, and so can being a nurse or a lawyer or an artist or a carpenter or an athlete or a retail store manager. It is not the specific job that matters, but how one does it. A job becomes a vocation when the work one does genuinely serves others and brings glory to God.

The Protestant idea of vocation translates into a practical spirituality that values self-discipline and industriousness. At the end of the day, Protestants are more likely to ask themselves what they have accomplished for God than to ponder whether they have somehow become more spiritual or emotionally closer to God. Most Protestants seek a warm personal relationship with God, but they also worry that emotions can mislead. For many Protestants, the expected pattern for spiritual growth follows a trajectory that leads from facts to faith to feelings. The facts of what God has done for humankind should elicit faith, and faith sometimes produces feelings of closeness to God. But if those feelings fail to materialize, this is not a matter of particular concern. For Protestants, feelings are optional.

The one venue for emotional expressiveness where Protestants have excelled is singing. Music has been a key part of Protestantism from the very beginning. Luther wrote songs and put them to music to help his followers maintain their fervor and to remind them of who they were (that is, not Catholic). He sometimes borrowed tunes from drinking songs because they were simple and easy to remember. Protestant singing is not limited to church. Protestants take their songs with them and sing them while traveling or at work. Many Protestant songs are vehicles for praising God, but their lyrics also provide religious comfort, strength, and encouragement. Some Protestant hymns are testimonies of personal experience. The most widely known Protestant hymn of this kind is *Amazing Grace*. Written by John Newton (1725–1807), a former slave trader who became an Anglican priest, the hymn charts his own conversion: "Amazing grace, how sweet the sound that saved a wretch like me! I once was lost but now am found, was blind but now I see."[3] More than two hundred years after it was written, this hymn still elicits powerful emotional reactions in many people who hear it. The greatest Protestant songwriter of all time, however, is undoubtedly Frances Jane ("Fanny") Crosby (1820–1915). Publishing her work under multiple pseudonyms, she composed roughly 8000 hymns during her lifetime. Some of her hymns, like "To God Be the Glory," are rousing anthems; others, like "Pass Me Not, O Gentle Savior," are plaintive cries of the heart.

Starting in the 1960s and 1970s, Protestant music began to change in many congregations as guitars and drums were added to (or replaced) organs and pianos as the instrumental accompaniment and as classical hymns sung from hymnbooks slowly gave way to newer praise songs with their lyrics often projected onto a screen at the front of the meeting room. Personal preferences for praise songs versus traditional hymns have sometimes sparked "worship wars" about which style of music to favor. Whatever form is preferred, vocal music remains a prominent part of Protestant culture, so much so that the beliefs and values of many Protestants derive as much from the songs they sing as from the Bible itself.

The Protestant Understanding of Salvation

Nothing was more important to early Protestants than getting salvation right. They were certain that Catholicism had gotten it wrong, and they saw it as their job to set the record straight. It seemed to them that Catholics had turned salvation into an institutional transaction, a commodity that could only be acquired through the Catholic Church. Protestants were intent on emphasizing the relational aspects of salvation instead. For Protestants, salvation is a personal encounter with God, a direct infusion of grace from God that establishes an unmediated relationship between the individual and the divine Redeemer. To caricature the difference between Catholicism and Protestantism, Catholics believe the Church is where one goes to obtain salvation, while Protestants believe the church is where people who are already saved gather together to worship God and learn more about their faith.

Early Protestants proposed a variety of theological views that diverged significantly from Catholic teaching. First and foremost, Protestants insisted that salvation is a free gift from God that has nothing to do with moral effort. Salvation is pure grace, and nothing else. Second, salvation happens all at once. It is instantaneous. A person either has salvation or not. Most Protestants acknowledge that the Christian life involves some elements of spiritual growth and moral maturation, but they chalk this up to a separate process called sanctification that follows salvation; it is not part of salvation itself. Finally, salvation is received by faith alone. Catholics believe that faith matters, but Catholics generally define faith as the God-given ability to assent to Christian truth as taught by the Church. Protestants champion a very different definition of faith. For Protestants, faith means trust, and the faith that brings salvation means entrusting one's entire life to God. Protestant faith is existential, not intellectual. It is a change of affectivity that alters people at the core of their being, enabling them to become, as Martin Luther once said, "joyful, confident, and happy with regard to God and all creatures."[4]

Early Protestants also disagreed with Catholics about the mechanics of salvation. How does salvation actually work? The Catholic tradition assumes that a person must be genuinely holy in order to enter heaven and stand in God's presence without shame. The sacraments help people to accumulate this kind of holiness, and purgatory allows Catholics to complete that process so they can enter heaven. Most Protestants deny the underlying premise that anyone can ever become wholly holy. Luther described the best a Christian can be as *simul justus et peccator*, always simultaneously a saint and a sinner. Yet, Protestants believe that imperfect people can still go to heaven. How is this possible? The Protestant answer is that Christians are clothed in the *imputed* righteousness of Christ so they appear holy in God's sight. For Protestants, salvation operates something like a legal ruling in a court of law. People stand before God (the judge) as guilty sinners, but Christ (humanity's advocate and defender) argues on their behalf that his own death on the cross paid the penalty for everyone's sins, so people can now be declared legally innocent as a result. This view of salvation keeps the focus clearly on Christ (not on human beings) and underscores Protestantism's separation of salvation from the pursuit of holiness and moral purity (sanctification).

The question naturally emerges: Who precisely gets to be declared legally innocent in God's sight, and how does this come about? Almost all the original Protestant reformers said that God makes this decision with no human involvement at all. God decides who gets saved and who does not. This position, which is especially associated with Reformed (or Calvinist) Protestantism, is called *predestination*, and its appeal arises from its alignment with the idea that salvation is a free and unearned gift from God. Over time, however, some Protestants began to wonder if predestination was compatible with Christianity's belief in a loving God. The Dutch theologian Jacob Arminius (1560–1609) reasoned that if God loves everyone, then surely salvation would be offered to everyone and it would be up to individuals to either accept or reject that offer. This position has been called *Arminianism* ever since. Today, a large majority of the world's Protestants have adopted an Arminian or "free will" explanation of salvation, but a third option, called *universalism*, is gaining ground. Universalism combines predestination's emphasis on God's choice with an Arminian emphasis on love and concludes that God has chosen to redeem everyone. For universalists, anything other than salvation for all would mean that sin can permanently block God's desire to redeem the world and everyone in it, which cannot be the case if God is omnipotent.

From their earliest days, Protestants have had differing opinions about whether and how much people can be assured of their own salvation. Faith is the key to salvation, but faith can waver. Even Martin Luther, the great champion of faith, had his doubts, and he sometimes found himself swinging violently between confidence and depression. Many Protestants seek to rectify this conundrum by linking faith to correct belief. For these Protestants, trust in God is salvific only if it is trust placed in who God really is. Correct belief is therefore essential to saving faith, and this conclusion can easily slide into an assumption that holding right beliefs about God guarantees salvation while holding mistaken or heretical views guarantees damnation. Other Protestants assume that living a good life and loving other people is the surest sign that one's faith is solid and one's salvation is secure. Living morally and loving others cannot themselves guarantee salvation, but they provide evidence of a changed heart. Still other Protestants think it is important to pinpoint a specific date and time when people "invited Christ into their heart" and were "born again." And finally, some Protestants believe their emotional sense of connection with God confirms their salvation. Along these lines, Charles Wesley, the founder of Methodism, once famously said that as he was sitting in church one day his heart was "strangely warmed" with feelings for God. In that single moment, he was convinced forever that his sins truly had been forgiven and he was saved indeed.[5]

For most of its history, Protestantism has defined salvation largely in terms of individuals and their eternal afterlife in either heaven or hell. Over the last century, however, this fixation on individuals and the afterlife has declined to some degree and belief in hell has declined dramatically. At the same time, more attention is being given to the social dimensions of both sin and salvation. Protestants now talk frequently about sin as embedded in institutions and social structures, and movements like the Social Gospel Movement, the Civil Rights Movement, and Christian feminism have focused on these kinds of communal and interpersonal concerns. If the concept of sin can be broadened to apply to institutions and communities as much as to individuals, it challenges the standard Protestant logic concerning salvation. Accordingly, some Protestants now argue that salvation applies to both individuals and groups and that the consequences of salvation are not limited to fellowship in the afterlife with God in heaven but also have an effect on the here-and-now of earthly existence.

Protestant History

Protestantism began in Europe during the early 1500s. It emerged suddenly, and for the first time in centuries Western European Christians were given a viable alternative to Catholicism. A number of earlier movements had presaged some of Protestantism's concerns – Waldensians in Italy, Wycliffites in England, and Hussites in Bohemia – but none of these groups permanently changed the European religious terrain. After the emergence of Protestantism, however, religion in Europe was never the same.

Protestantism did not have a lone charismatic trailblazer. It was a movement with many leaders, and Protestant ideas and aspirations spread quickly and widely throughout Europe. The dispersion of Protestant views was aided enormously by the invention of the moveable type printing press, which allowed Protestant pamphlets to be published with unprecedented speed. The rise of European nationalism also assisted Protestantism since some political leaders welcomed the new movement as a mechanism for lessening the social power of the Catholic Church and for seizing some of the Church's wealth. In the end, however, Protestantism seems to have succeeded largely because of its spiritual appeal. Thousands of Europeans had become dissatisfied with the Catholicism of the day. They were looking for something else, and they found that something in Protestantism.

Protestantism's Diverse Origins, 1500 to 1650

Martin Luther (1483–1546) was one of the earliest and most visible leaders of the Protestant movement. Both a priest and a professor of theology at the University of Wittenberg in northern Germany, Luther published his famous 95

Theses that condemned the Catholic practice of selling indulgences (certificates promising to reduce a person's suffering in purgatory) in 1517, and by 1520 his views on purgatory and many other matters had been disseminated across the continent. In response, Pope Leo X excommunicated him, and the Holy Roman Emperor Charles V labeled him an outlaw. Fortunately for Luther, he had political friends in high places who protected him from prosecution. In the years that followed, Luther married a former nun named Katarina von Bora and became the father of six children. He also wrote and published more books, essays, sermons, and letters than almost anyone in history. By the time of his death in 1546, Lutheran Protestantism had become the dominant form of Christianity in Scandinavia and in most of northern Germany.

Other varieties of Protestantism popped up elsewhere. In the mid-1520s, the Anabaptist movement developed in Switzerland and the Low Countries (Belgium, Luxembourg, and the Netherlands) and proposed a set of reforms that were even more radical than Luther. Anabaptists only baptize adults who are capable of making religious decisions for themselves, and they are also pacifists, which made them dangerous to political leaders in need of an army. They were persecuted by Catholic and Protestant rulers alike. A decade later, John Calvin (1509–1564) articulated a new form of Protestantism that focused almost entirely on correct doctrine. Operating out of Geneva, Switzerland, Calvin and his associates vigorously promoted their views across the continent, and Calvinist perceptions of God, Christ, sin, salvation, and the Church have remained key points of reference for Protestants ever since, especially within Presbyterian and Reformed circles.

Across the Channel in England, Christianity was declared to be post-Catholic by King Henry VIII in 1535, but his motives were not particularly theological. Henry wanted a divorce and the pope refused to approve it, so he broke with Rome and created a new Church of England with himself in charge. While it was now independent, Henry's Church was still largely Catholic in beliefs and practice. Almost immediately, some British Protestants began trying to make the church more explicitly and consistently Protestant. A few, including a contingent of Baptists, eventually abandoned the Church of England over differences regarding doctrine and church practice. The Church of England was gradually de-catholicized, but it never became unambiguously Protestant. Even today, some Anglicans think of themselves and their church as existing in its own unique space at the intersection of Catholicism and Protestantism.

From the start, Europe's Catholic rulers perceived Protestantism not merely as a menace to the Catholic Church but also as a political threat. The entire continent soon was embroiled in a prolonged cycle of violence fueled by religious differences. After roughly a century of fighting, hostilities abated and a pragmatic peace took hold. The political solution, known as the Peace of Westphalia (1648), produced a checkerboard of regional state churches. Each local kingdom, duchy, principality, or nation could choose its own preferred faith – either Catholicism or some form of Protestantism – which became that locale's one and only approved religion. Lutheranism was chosen as the state-designated religion in Scandinavia and northern Germany, the Church of England became the state religion in England and Wales, and Calvinist Protestantism became the dominant faith in Scotland and in various sections of Germany, Switzerland, Hungary, and Romania. For a time, Protestantism also flourished in parts of Poland and France, but by 1650 the religious map of Western Europe had come to look very much like it still appears today (see Figure 4.2).

Three New Protestant Spiritual Orientations, 1650–1800

During the years from 1650 to 1800, Protestantism's identity was made more complex by the emergence of three new spiritual orientations that crisscrossed the religio-geographic lines of difference created by the Peace of Westphalia. *Confessionalism*, the most widely dispersed of these new spiritual dispositions, focused on the clarity and precision of beliefs. The second orientation was *pietism*, often called *revivalism* in North America, which stressed the importance of religious experience (especially conversion) and discipleship (moral purity and service to others). Finally, some Protestants became convinced that the

Figure 4.2 Religious map of Catholic and Protestant Europe c. 1650. (Regions colored white were predominantly Orthodox).

concerns of faith were best served through *rationalism,* which means thinking logically and scientifically about God, oneself, and the universe. Confessionalism, pietism, and rationalism still exist as powerful influences within Protestantism today, shaping attitudes and practices around the world.

Protestants with a confessional bent think it is crucial to articulate Christian beliefs as clearly and definitively as possible. To this end, they have developed various Protestant creeds and confessions of faith that outline correct doctrine in short and concise formulas, and they have also produced long works of systematic theology that explain all the details and implications of these creeds. Protestantism stressed correct doctrine from its very beginning, and confessionalism took up that task with great enthusiasm. Even when only theologians and church leaders could understand all the implications and nuance of these statements of faith, many Protestant laypeople still found it reassuring that at least someone knew what was genuinely true and what wasn't. Even today, confessional Protestants continue to emphasize the importance of right belief and are eager to point out errors in the beliefs of others.

Confessionalists pay scant attention to religious experience and emotions, but experience and emotions are at the heart of a second Protestant spiritual orientation called *pietism.* The German Lutheran minister Philip Jakob Spener (1635–1705) was an early leader of the movement and spelled out its emphases in his book *Pia Desideria* (*Pious Longings*). Rather than focusing on doctrine, pietistic Protestants stress faithful living; instead of arguing over Christian beliefs, they devote their time to prayer, Bible study, moral self-discipline, and serving the needs of others. Pietists place great emphasis on the personal experience of conversion. In North America, where pietism was often called revivalism, supporters of the movement sometimes held special public meetings (called "revivals") where dramaturgical preaching – it was said that the revivalist preacher George Whitefield could bring people to tears merely by pronouncing the word "Mesopotamia" – and the emotional fervor of the crowd helped individuals to overcome their spiritual inhibitions and turn their lives over to God.

In Europe, most pietists remained members of their respective state churches and expressed their pietistic sentiments in smaller gatherings held during the week with other like-minded believers. However, some pietists eventually became disillusioned with the state church system and created their own independent "free" churches, places that were free from any association with the state and where they could worship God as they pleased. The most prominent example of separatist pietism is Methodism, which began as a devotional movement within the Church of England but eventually split away, first in the United States and later in England itself. As the Methodist Church slowly lost its emotional fervor over the years, some members branched off from Methodism to create a host of new experience-oriented churches and denominations that became known collectively as the Holiness Movement. Free church movements in Scandinavia and Germany had a different origin and tone. Often developed out of Lutheranism, they sometimes used the phrase "higher life" to describe themselves, and they tended to be more subdued in their spirituality than the boisterous Holiness churches that emerged from Methodism.

Rationalism, the third new Protestant orientation, thought that confessionalism's focus on dogma was misplaced and that pietism's emphasis on the emotions was anti-intellectual. What rational Protestants wanted instead was an intelligent faith focused on understanding the world and then doing what was right. Often associated with Deism in the English-speaking world, Protestant rationalists believed that Christianity's core message was relatively simple and that any clear-thinking person could discover it whether they were Christians or not. Rational Protestants thought the Bible was an important guide for life, but they also believed rational interpretation was required to separate its moral gold from the quasi-magical context in which it was often embedded. Rationalism was far less pervasive than either confessionalism or pietism during the seventeenth and eighteenth centuries, but it blossomed during the nineteenth century. Today, progressive Protestantism continues to stress the moral rather than the distinctively spiritual or supernatural dimensions of biblical faith.

World Missions and Modern Knowledge, 1800–1950

Given the fervor with which Protestants express their faith, it is somewhat surprising that they showed almost no interest in sharing their convictions with people outside of Europe during the first 300 years of the movement. This lackadaisical attitude toward world missions was directly challenged in 1792 when a British Baptist by the name of William Carey published a bombshell book, entitled *Enquiry into the Obligations of Christians to Use Means for the Conversion of the Heathens*. Completely dismissing the predestinarian objection that God could redeem "the heathen" without human assistance if God were so inclined, Carey urged Protestants to use *means* – intelligent and well-planned action – to spread the gospel around the world.

Carey was only one of many Protestant missionaries who set out to save lives and change the world. Many of these Protestant missionaries traveled abroad with the support of their home denominations, but Protestants also organized a wide variety of new independent or interdenominational agencies to carry out the work of world evangelism. These new voluntary associations supported many male missionaries, but they also funded the missionary efforts of many Protestant women. Some, like the Woman's Union Missionary Society, founded by Sarah Platt Doremus in New York City in 1861, were entirely dedicated to this work. By the end of the century, the image of the fearless, single missionary woman had reshaped Protestant expectations of what women could and should be. Women generally had more freedom and support within pietistic Protestant circles than in either the confessional or rational wings of the movement.

The modern Protestant missionary movement was a massive undertaking, and it was often aided by Europe's contemporaneous colonization of the world. Wherever European colonialists went, Protestant missionaries were sure to follow, and in time American missionaries also joined their ranks. The gospel preached by Protestant missionaries combined Christianity with Western culture, thoroughly blending Western attitudes about cleanliness, education, ethics, time-consciousness, dress, and self-discipline with Christian notions of sin, salvation, faith, and the Bible. But while their message was thoroughly Western, Protestant missionaries also taught local converts how to read and interpret the Bible for themselves, giving them the means to criticize whatever the missionaries said. And millions of converts in Africa and Asia (Protestantism never made any significant inroads in Latin America) did just that, producing their own new versions of Christianity that often differed significantly from the Western-style Protestantism of the missionaries.

While European, and later American, Protestant missionaries were spreading their version of the gospel around the world, Protestants back home were continuing to reconsider, revise, and defend their own faith, often in response to new intellectual developments and scientific theories. Darwinian biology, socialist economics, Freudian psychology, and other innovative perspectives raised questions about many traditional Christian beliefs, and reactions tended to flow in two opposite directions. One group of Protestants, originally called either modernists or liberals, welcomed these new academic insights as a means of refining and deepening their faith commitments. Another group of Protestants, known as fundamentalists or conservatives, argued that these new ideas, which often contradicted the literal meaning of the Bible, ought to be rejected as erroneous and heretical. Both attitudes are still observable in Protestantism today.

Global Protestant Dynamics, 1950 to the Present

After World War II, Protestantism became fully global. A third of the world's Protestants now live in Africa, a quarter are found in North America, 20 percent reside in Asia, and only about 15 percent remain in Europe. Missionary activity continues, but it is no longer one-sided. While Europe and the United States continue to send missionaries abroad, a host of other countries, including Brazil, Nigeria, and South Korea, have also become major Protestant missionary-sending nations. This new trend, which is sometimes called "reverse mission," is so large that the United States has now become the world's top receiver of missionaries as well as its top sender. Protestantism is also being spread around the globe by migration. Whether this involves the temporary migration of businesspeople, guest workers, and refugees or is a permanent relocation, the movement of massive numbers of people is changing the global Protestant profile. Different kinds of Protestants from different parts of the world are now interacting with each other more frequently than ever before.

Protestantism has been deeply affected by changing political and moral norms around the globe, and concerns related to race and gender have become especially prominent. Slavery ended in the nineteenth century, but racial prejudice has continued to infect many communities of white Protestants. Today only a tiny percentage of Protestants condone overt racism, but it took the American Civil Rights movement of the 1950s and 1960s and the South African anti-apartheid movement of the late twentieth century to establish racial equality as the Protestant norm. Gender equality is another matter of contention within contemporary Protestantism. The first battles focused on the ordination of women. Only a miniscule number of Protestant women were ordained before the 1970s. Since then, many Protestant churches have opened their pulpits to women, but numerous Protestant churches, including the massive Southern Baptist Convention in the United States, still ban women from the pulpit. In recent years, questions about the membership status and ordination possibilities for LGBTQ individuals have also become flashpoints of division within the Protestant world. Some Protestant churches now welcome LGBTQ persons as members, but few allow ordination, and most Protestant churches worldwide continue to condemn LGBTQ behavior as immoral.

Since the 1950s, the divide that emerged in the early twentieth century between modernists and fundamentalists has morphed into a broader conflict between progressive Protestantism and evangelical Protestantism. The divide is no longer focused on science as much as on other more practical matters related to Christian life and ethics. Social justice and inclusivity have become central concerns for progressives. For them, being Christian means making the world a more just and equitable place for everyone and welcoming people into fellowship regardless of where they may be on life's journey. Progressive Protestant congregations and denominations continue to affirm the vast majority of Protestantism's historic beliefs, but they are not particularly concerned about church doctrine. They see faith as dynamic and doubts as unavoidable. What is non-negotiable, however, is the Golden Rule of loving God and others.

Evangelicalism is the other major strand of contemporary Protestantism. Historically, the United States has been the worldwide center of evangelicalism, but it has become a global movement. Evangelicals were originally united by their conservative theology and their desire to share the gospel with everyone on earth, but a political element has been inserted in recent years, focusing especially on the protection of "traditional values" related to family, gender, and sexuality. Many evangelicals also embrace a dispensational view of history which assumes that the world is entering the "end times" when Christ will return to earth to "rapture" the church (take all true Christians immediately to heaven) and then to judge everyone who is "left behind." The evangelical movement has deep roots in both confessionalism and pietism. Evangelicalism's confessional disposition is evident in its continuing emphasis on right doctrine; its pietistic and experiential orientation is visible in its increasing affinity with Pentecostalism. In fact, global evangelicalism today is no longer a purely Protestant movement; Pentecostal Christians and conservative Protestants are equally likely to refer to themselves as evangelicals.

Institutional and Social Structure of Protestantism

The institutional structure of Protestantism is far different from that of Catholicism and Orthodoxy. The other two traditions are housed in easily identifiable church institutions. Protestantism is, by contrast, a movement, and it is housed in many different organizations, associations, and social networks. If the traditions of Catholicism and Orthodoxy are imagined as parades of people marching in formation down two different well-marked streets, then Protestantism is more like a herd of cattle wandering in roughly the same direction across an unmarked field. Protestants have a common ethos and they share some key theological convictions, but these commonalities percolate from the ground up rather than flowing from the top down, and there is no shared institutional framework to connect or coordinate all the activity.

Protestantism's long history of ecclesiastical diversity and theological creativity can, however, make the movement appear to be more disorganized than it really is. As a counterpoint, it is helpful to remember that two-thirds of the world's Protestants are associated with just five church clusters: Anglican, Baptist, Lutheran, Methodist, and Reformed (including Presbyterians). All five of these Protestant groups have organized themselves into separate global fellowships, and together they have a worldwide membership of more than 350 million (see Table 4.1). Most other Protestants belong to one of five additional groups: Baptists who are not associated with the Baptist World Alliance; Wesleyan Holiness churches (like the Nazarenes and the Church of God); self-designated "primitivist" churches (like the Christian Churches and Churches of Christ); Anabaptist and historic peace churches (like the Mennonites, Brethren, and Quakers); and a sizeable group of smaller denominations, church associations, and independent congregations that embrace a "nondenominational" or "inter-denominational" identity. These ten categories do not include every Protestant church or denomination, but they comfortably account for more than 95 percent of all Protestants worldwide.

Table 4.1 Five major Protestant families, representing two-thirds of all Protestants worldwide.

Family name	Global organization (year founded)	Number of denominations represented	Number of countries represented	Number of global adherents
Anglican	Anglican Communion (1931)	46	165	85,000,000
Baptist	Baptist World Alliance (1905)	239	125	50,000,000
Lutheran	Lutheran World Federation (1947)	148	89	75,000,000
Methodist	World Methodist Council (1881)	80	138	80,000,000
Reformed	World Alliance of Reformed Churches (1970)	218	100	75,000,000

Looking at Protestantism from an even more distant perspective, it is possible to simplify the picture further. Globally, Protestantism can be divided in two: some Protestants belong to European-style state churches; other Protestants are members of American-style independent denominations.

Almost all of the earliest Protestant communities followed the state–church model, with Anabaptism being a noteworthy exception. Protestantism's alliance with the state was initially largely pragmatic; the movement needed political protection in order to survive. However, the European state–church system also has a theological rationale: it ensures the proper worship of God and it requires all the Christians in a given region to cooperate with each other. In the sixteenth and seventeenth centuries, most European state churches assumed that they were mandated to exercise monopolistic control over all legal religious activity in their territories of oversight. This is no longer true; these institutions have evolved. Now most of Europe's old state churches have morphed into "folk churches" that see themselves as serving the spiritual needs of everyone in the societies where they are located. In the past, state church pastors often felt obligated to tell people what they were supposed to believe, but today's folk church pastors function much more like chaplains who seek to help their parishioners in their spiritual journeys wherever those journeys may be heading. This shift of focus has led some scholars to liken Europe's contemporary Protestant folk churches to public utilities: they exist to provide religious services to anyone who needs or wants those services, but they do not intrude where they are not invited. Because of this public orientation, most of these churches still receive at least some tax-supported funding from the state.

Apart from their public function, many folk church leaders would argue that their churches also represent what any truly Christian church ought to be: places that preach and that worship a non-parochial God who genuinely loves and cares for everyone. From a folk church perspective, the aggressive competitiveness associated with America's more freewheeling, non-state-affiliated style of Protestantism makes each separate denomination inherently prone to claim God for themselves. This makes God look like a tribal deity, who loves one group of people more than others, rather than like the Creator of the universe. The great challenge facing European folk church Protestants is that a wide swath of Europeans no longer feel any need for their services. Many Europeans no longer believe in God and most younger Europeans have only rarely, if ever, been in a church building. Churches are often treated as if they are merely curious relics from the past. If the public understanding of Christianity deteriorates any further, making a convincing argument for the continued existence of these churches may become difficult.

In contrast to the state–church model, a far different, more entrepreneurial style of Protestantism developed in the United States and has subsequently spread around the globe. When the United States declared its independence in 1776, it was already home to a wide variety of different Protestant churches. No one wanted someone else's church to be religiously in charge of the nation, so the pragmatic framers of the Constitution mandated separation of church and state. Religion was relegated to operating in an open marketplace, and churches had to compete for members and financial support. The purpose of a Protestant church in America is not to serve the whole "folk" of the nation, but to serve its own members. There is also a deeper theological rationale for America's choice-oriented style of Protestantism. Most Americans believe that faith is genuine only if it is freely chosen; they are convinced that coercion of any kind subverts authentic faith. Given this theological inclination, the only church that makes sense is one that is entirely voluntary and free from any connection to the state.

Despite the diversity of American Protestantism, there has historically been a great deal of agreement across the American churches regarding public standards and values. Even though these churches have, in one sense, been competing against each other, they have also, in another sense, seen each other as partners in faith. This mixture of competition and camaraderie is the key to what Americans call *denominationalism*. In essence, American-style Protestantism rejects the notion of heresy and views other churches as merely having different sets of emphases. Members of other churches are not religious enemies; they are merely competitors in a free market of religious productivity.

American-style Protestantism faces a very different set of challenges than folk church Protestantism. Denominations and individual congregations can easily become enclaves of like-mindedness, and many Protestant churches both in America and around the world now act as echo chambers that reinforce the religious (and other) prejudices of members. In America, people are prone to join or leave Protestant churches based on how well their spiritual whims of the moment are being met. People attend a church (often with no intention of formally joining) because they like the choir or because the pastor is a good preacher or because the congregation has a good youth program, but if any of these things alter, or if their own prefer-ences change, then they go looking for another church home. This is called church shopping, and many Protestants around the world have become adept church shoppers. There was a time in the past when Protestant denominations elicited a high degree of loyalty from members, but much of that loyalty has disappeared.

For many Protestants, their most meaningful institutional connections are not with a church or denomination, but with one or another parachurch organ-ization. The term "parachurch" refers to any group or voluntary religious asso-ciation that seeks to advance some Christian cause without itself becoming a full-fledged church. Parachurch organizations do not usually baptize people, serve communion, marry people, or bury them, and the individuals who lead these groups are often laypeople rather than ordained pastors. Some of the old-est Protestant parachurch organizations were Bible societies (that supported the distribution of Bibles), missionary societies, and associations for youth, like the YMCA (the Young Men's Christian Association) which was founded in 1844. More recently, Protestant parachurch organizations often focus on social and humanitarian needs, including groups like World Vision (founded in 1950) and Habitat for Humanity (founded in 1976). Many Protestant publishing houses and media corporations, which are for-profit businesses, also operate similarly to parachurch ministries, trying to aid and advance Protestant Christianity around the globe. Protestant parachurch organizations share many characteristics with Catholicism's new ecclesiastical movements (NEMs), and both kinds of organizations point toward the increasing activism of Christian laypeople worldwide.

Protestantism has changed significantly during its 500-year history. It began as a movement that was heavily dependent on political assistance for its sur-vival and slowly became an independent, self-sustaining, and democratic move-ment. Before Protestantism existed, Christianity placed little emphasis on choice. People were born into different Christian communities and that is where they typically stayed. But once Protestants injected the notion of choice into Christianity, the preferences of individuals often took precedence over tra-dition. This shift of emphasis has impacted all of Christianity, not just Protestantism, and it has also deeply shaped ideas about freedom and individu-ality in Western culture as a whole.

Notes

1 "John Robinson's Farewell Sermon," https://pilgrimhall.org/pdf/John_ Robinson_Farewell_Sermon.pdf (accessed 15 May 2020).

2 Reuben A. Torrey, *The Christ of the Bible* (New York: George H. Doran, 1924), p. 14.

3 "Amazing Grace" lyrics, https://www.hymnal.net/en/hymn/h/313 (accessed November 7, 2020).

4 Martin Luther, *Preface to the Letter of St. Paul to the Romans* (1522), available online at https://history.hanover.edu/courses/excerpts/111luth2.html (accessed May 24, 2020).

5 John Wesley, *Journal of John Wesley*, chapter 2, Christian Classics Ethereal Library, https://www.ccel.org/ccel/wesley/journal.vi.ii.xvi.html (accessed July 15, 2019).

5

Pentecostalism

The Power of the Spirit

Pentecostalism is so recent in origin that the movement's name is still unsettled. Sometimes it is called "charismatic" (because it stresses the "charisms" or "gifts" of the Holy Spirit), sometimes it is called "renewalist" (because it renews faith that has become dull or routine), and sometimes it is called "Spirit-filled" (because it emphasizes the Holy Spirit). Regardless of the name, what distinguishes this tradition is its focus on having a personal, miraculous experience of God's presence in one's life. The word "Pentecostal," which is used here, is the oldest and most common way of naming the movement, and it is derived from the New Testament's description of the Holy Spirit's descent on the followers of Jesus on the day of Pentecost several weeks after Christ's death. According to the Book of Acts, the Holy Spirit rushed into the room where the group was meeting, sounding like a mighty wind and looking like flames of fire.

In the New Testament story about that original day of Pentecost, Jesus's disciples were miraculously empowered by their reception of the Holy Spirit and left the meeting speaking excitedly in ways that other people heard as either a variety of different human languages or as drunken rambling. When the modern Pentecostal movement burst onto the scene at the beginning of the twentieth century, a similar phenomenon was reported by the *Los Angeles Daily Times* with a headline screaming "Weird Babel of Tongues."[1] Speaking in tongues was so central to early Pentecostalism that it was sometimes referred to as the "tongues movement."

Since that headline announcing the Pentecostal meetings in Los Angeles just over a century ago, the growth of Pentecostalism has been phenomenal. Almost a fifth of the world's Christians now identify with the movement. Pentecostals themselves would say that this growth has been brought about by the Holy Spirit, but social conditions have also fueled the explosion of Spirit-filled Christianity around the world and especially among the world's poor. More than any other Christian tradition, Pentecostalism allows people who have been beaten down by the world to feel loved and empowered by God – and the emphasis on feeling is important. Pentecostal Christians don't just believe in

What Is Christianity? First Edition. Douglas Jacobsen.
© 2022 John Wiley & Sons Ltd. Published 2022 by John Wiley & Sons Ltd.

God; they claim to feel God's presence physically in their bodies. The popularity of Pentecostalism is aided by the fact that its practices are inexpensive. Pentecostals do not need cathedrals or icons, and they do not require highly trained clergy. All that is necessary for worship is to lift hands and voices in praise of God, and this action can occur anywhere, including in the shabbiest of settings. Partly because it offers so much for so little, Pentecostalism has become the fastest-growing religious movement in the history of the world.

Many Pentecostal Christians are poor, and some sociologists have described Pentecostalism as a religion of the oppressed, claiming that it functions as a spiritual coping mechanism for people dealing with social and economic distress. But not all Pentecostals are poor, and most Pentecostal Christians who are poor would reject that description of themselves. While they might readily admit that faith helps them to endure the harshness of life, they would more emphatically say that it also energizes them with a sense of power and purpose. The Holy Spirit gives them the ability to bind demons, to heal the sick, to live at peace with their neighbors, and when necessary to stand up for their own rights. When they hear God's call to action, received through dreams, visions, and prophetic utterances as well as through the words of the Bible, it gives them a sense of divine leading and guidance. Rather than being the passive poor who need God's help merely to survive, most Pentecostal Christians see themselves as God's agents who have been charged with transforming the world through the power of God's Spirit.

Pentecostal Spirituality

Pentecostal spirituality centers on experience: feeling God's presence within one's own body. The testimonies of millions of Pentecostal Christians describe feeling overwhelmed by a strange and wonderful power when the Spirit of God came into their lives. The early Pentecostal leader William Durham gave a detailed report of his own experience:

> I was overcome by the mighty fulness of power and went down under it. For three hours [the Spirit of God] wrought wonderfully in me. My body was worked in sections, a section at a time. And even the skin on my face was jerked and shaken, and finally I felt my lower jaw begin to quiver in a strange way. This continued for some little time, when finally my throat began to enlarge and I felt my vocal organs being, as it were, drawn into a different shape. O how strange and wonderful it was! and how blessed it was to be thus in the hands of God. And last of all I felt my tongue begin to move and my lips to produce strange sounds which did not originate in my mind.[2]

Another early Pentecostal leader said more succinctly that the Pentecostal experience was like swallowing "God liquidized."[3] It went down easy and changed everything.

Because feelings play such a large role in Pentecostalism, some Pentecostals have argued that what makes their movement distinctive is its emphasis on "orthopathy" (right feelings) in contrast to orthodoxy (right belief) or orthopraxy (right behavior). Pentecostals feel God, while other Christians just think about God or try to do what God wants. Pentecostal Christians do indeed emphasize experience and emotions, but it would be a mistake to characterize Pentecostalism as solely experiential or affective. Pentecostal theologians can parse their words with as much skill and nuance as any Catholic or Protestant. Nonetheless, Pentecostals share a fundamental agreement with Orthodoxy: words can sometimes be helpful, but they ultimately fail. God is more magnificent, and the world is far stranger, than words or rationality can ever fully comprehend.

Some people think of the Pentecostal movement as a new kind of Protestantism, and they are reluctant to identify Pentecostalism as a fourth major Christian tradition. There are good reasons for this hesitancy. Like Protestantism, Pentecostalism stresses the individual's relationship with God and the importance of the Bible, and like Protestantism it has no central leadership structure. It is also undeniable that Pentecostalism is linked historically to Protestantism and more specifically to the pietistic strand of Protestant faith and life. In this regard, the relationship between Protestantism and Pentecostalism is probably best compared to the relationship that existed between Orthodoxy and Catholicism around the year 900. At that point in time there was still a great deal of overlap between Catholicism and Orthodoxy, but their core spiritualities had begun to drift apart and they were well on their way to becoming separate and distinct traditions. The same kind of differentiation now seems to be taking place between Protestantism and Pentecostalism. Perhaps this phase is temporary, and the two movements will ultimately merge again, but currently each group is distinct.

Pentecostalism's focus is on the Spirit, on empirically *experiencing* God beyond or outside the realm of words. This spiritual orientation is very different from Protestantism's emphasis on the Word, on *understanding* God's message as it was communicated to humanity through the Bible. Rather than construing faith as a matter of the mind, Pentecostals pay attention to the heart. Pentecostalism is about being enveloped in the love of God. It is about being healed emotionally and physically by God's presence. It is about being "slain in the Spirit" (knocked unconscious by God's power). It is about "letting go and letting God," shutting off one's thinking and relaxing into the flow of God's Spirit within and around one's body. Self-control is a Protestant virtue, but for Pentecostal Christians it is precisely the willingness to sometimes lose control that allows one to experience God authentically.

William Durham's description of losing control under the power of the Spirit concludes with his lips producing "strange sounds which did not originate in my mind." This is a reference to speaking in tongues, and Pentecostals consider speaking in tongues to be a gift of the Holy Spirit that helps them communicate with God. For some Pentecostal groups, speaking in tongues is also the sign that an individual has received the *baptism with the Holy Spirit*, by which a person is completely filled with the Holy Spirit and receives new spiritual power.

Today, speaking in tongues is optional in many Pentecostal circles. A singular emphasis on the gift of tongues has given way to a wider appreciation of all the gifts of the Holy Spirit, including both the miraculous (such as claims to heal the sick, predict the future, or even raise the dead) and the relatively ordinary (such as the ability to teach or lead or encourage others). A similar moderation of opinion has taken place regarding the notion of the baptism with the Holy Spirit. While many Pentecostals still consider this experience to be unique and necessary – it is the visible marker that proves and validates one's Pentecostal faith – many members of the broader Pentecostal movement now assume that a person can arrive at the Spirit-filled life via different pathways, not all of them linked to a specific experience identified as the baptism with the Spirit.

Pentecostal Christians live with the miraculous, and they assume that God's wonder-working power should be part of the ordinary Christian life. Individuals in all the Christian traditions (and most of the world's religions) believe that miracles sometimes take place, but Pentecostal Christians assume that miracles occur all the time. They believe that God is constantly watching over human-kind and that God is ready and willing to intervene even in the smallest details of life. So Pentecostal believers pray and expect God to respond, whether they are requesting a good parking spot, yearning for a child to be healed from ter-minal cancer, pleading for a hurricane to be directed away from the city where they live, or seeking reconciliation when a friendship has been broken. Nothing is too small or too big to bring to God in prayer.

Pentecostals know that God does not answer all prayers in the way they want those prayers to be answered. Pentecostals lose their jobs, their marriages fall apart, tornados hit their homes, banks in which they put their money fail, they get sick, and they die. But sometimes God does seem to intervene, and when that happens, Pentecostal Christians tell each other about it. They *testify* about what God has done for them, and if one person begins to testify then others almost always begin to tell their stories too. People love stories – it is part of being human – and people remember and retell the stories they have heard, especially if those stories are sources of encouragement and hope. So, amid life's sorrows, Pentecostals share their miracle stories and remind each other that God loves them regardless of circumstances and that somehow, even in the worst of times, God can miraculously turn sadness and evil into good. When bad things happen, the Pentecostal reaction is not to doubt God's power, but instead to cling to God's love, waiting to see how God will eventually bring blessing out of adversity. And when life is good, that too is all because of God.

Most Pentecostal Christians assume that they are involved in a massive invisible spiritual battle. Angels and demons clash around them, and Christians are called to join in the fray against the forces of evil. This is not meant as a metaphor. Most Pentecostal Christians believe the world is literally infested with evil spirits intent on doing harm. Some Pentecostals believe the world has been parceled out by Satan to various subsidiary territorial demons who are intent on undermining God's will for different specific regions of the world. Pentecostals must accordingly always be on their guard, especially since Satan and his minions can disguise themselves as angels of light and attack through deception. Pentecostals can be predisposed to conspiracy thinking, but that very same way of thinking can sometimes help them to unmask evil in the world (social and economic as well as spiritual) that might otherwise proceed without notice or impediment.

Many Pentecostals believe they are living in "the last days" and that the battle with evil is becoming more intense. In the power of the Spirit and Jesus's name, Pentecostal Christians are committed to binding the forces of evil and setting individuals free from spiritual captivity. For modern people who believe the world consists solely of what can be observed and measured, the Pentecostal approach can sound like nonsensical fantasy. But the great majority of the world's people, including many people in the purportedly modern West, still believe in demons, evil spirits, and the haunting presence of the dead. In such a world, the message of Pentecostal power can become literally a godsend, a promise of desperately needed protection that frees them from spiritual fear, perhaps for the first time in their lives.

A large majority of the world's Pentecostal Christians are women. This can be explained in part by Pentecostalism's assumption that the Holy Spirit can empower women in the same way that the Spirit empowers men. For Pentecostals, everyone is equal in the Spirit. This theological assumption of spiritual equality has not, however, always led to equality in church practices. Pentecostalism can be as patriarchal as any other Christian tradition. Even in the most patriarchal Pentecostal churches, however, women have never been fully subservient. Pentecostal women know that God can use them to do great things, and they have often assumed prominent roles. Perhaps the most famous is Aimee Semple McPherson, whose popularity in early twentieth-century America rivaled that of the hottest stars of Hollywood. She was a flamboyant performer (see Figure 5.1), but she was also socially concerned. Her church provided free meals for thousands of hungry people during the Great Depression in the 1930s.

Figure 5.1 Aimee Semple McPherson (front row, second from left) in a performance at her church, Angelus Temple, in Los Angeles. *Source*: SteamWiki, https://en.wikipedia.org/wiki/File:LAPL_ASM_Performance00021729.jpg

For many women, Pentecostalism's appeal may also be related to its domestic influence. Simply put, Pentecostalism frequently improves life at home. Many Pentecostal churches teach that the husband is to be the head of the home, but men are also required to be faithful and kind. In patriarchal societies where male domination is a way of life, placing that kind of moral responsibility on husbands can be a huge step forward. Many wives will gladly obey their husbands if their husbands will stop spending their earnings on alcohol, stop their extramarital affairs, and become faithful spouses and responsible fathers. If marital difficulties arise, Pentecostal couples can ascribe the fault to Satan rather than to each other, and they can join forces to fight Satan together and save their marriages simultaneously.

Pentecostal Christianity emphasizes the miraculous and the supernatural, but perhaps the key characteristic that distinguishes it from other Christian traditions is something quite simple and ordinary: joy. Pentecostal believers say they feel joy in the presence of God, and they express that joy in the exuberance of their worship. Catholic and Orthodox liturgies and Protestant Sunday worship services can sometimes seem dry, dull, and somber with members attending grudgingly as a religious duty. But in Pentecostal worship, people dance and sing, they clap their hands, they shout, they march around the room, they hug each other, they "get happy in the Lord," and they rejoice. Pentecostal believers know how to cry – in fact, tears are considered a spiritual gift – but the predominant emotion is joy. Awash in joy, Pentecostal Christians do not attend church reluctantly or out of a sense of duty; they go to church happily and willingly because it is fun. That sense of holy fun goes a long way toward explaining not only how the Pentecostal movement differs from other Christian traditions, but also why it has grown so rapidly.

The Pentecostal Understanding of Salvation

In the Pentecostal tradition, salvation has a focus on the future. Pentecostals assume that salvation entails the forgiveness of past sins and the righting of past wrongs, but the attention of Pentecostal Christians is directed toward what is yet to come, on the blessings that God has yet in store for those who believe. This perspective has more in common with Orthodoxy's focus on deification (in the future) than it does with Catholicism and Protestantism's stress on sin and for-giveness (faults in the past). The word *fullness*, a term that allows for ever more expansion, is sometimes used to communicate that salvation is future-oriented and concerned with growth-in-godliness. Salvation is not just about forgiveness, nor is it only about holiness understood as the absence of sin, and it is not some-thing that is simply done once and then is complete. Instead, salvation for the Pentecostal tradition is a matter of faith in motion, of moving ever deeper into the fullness of God and into the fullness of life that God intends for everyone.

Yet salvation in the Pentecostal tradition is still distinctly tied to the present. Pentecostals often remark that there is "healing in the atonement," meaning that Christ's crucifixion and resurrection somehow address humanity's physi-cal and physiological necessities as well as spiritual needs. In the early years of the Pentecostal movement, some leaders instructed their followers to avoid all use of modern medicine because healing was supposed to come directly from God. Visiting a doctor was construed as lack of faith, and some extreme groups drank poison or tossed around venomous snakes to demonstrate that God would protect them. Over the years, the level of stridency about healing has decreased. Most Pentecostal Christians today believe that God usually brings healing through a combination of modern medicine and faith. A famous mid-twentieth-century Pentecostal healer, Kathryn Kuhlman, helped the movement make this transition. She constantly told the crowds that flooded into her meet-ings: "I believe that God has the power to heal instantly...but I also believe that God gave us our brains to use!"[4] Kuhlman believed in divine healing, but she also believed in doctors and modern medicine.

A blurring together of physical and spiritual needs is also characteristic of the so-called *prosperity gospel* which is currently a prominent aspect of global Pentecostalism. Every week, literally thousands of Spirit-filled preachers tell their followers that God wants them not only to be spiritually redeemed and physically healed, but also to be financially blessed. The standard message goes something like this: if people want a nice house or a new car or fashionable clothing, they have the right to claim those things in Jesus's name. Claiming those blessings requires faith, however, and the kind of convinced faith that is necessary is typically demonstrated by donating some kind of "seed offering" to the preacher's own church. That seed offering, which is often a substantial portion of a poor person's total assets, shows God the sincerity of a person's faith, and God then responds – some preachers say God is obligated to respond – by granting that individual a bountiful harvest of wealth.

Obviously, there is tremendous potential for charlatanism within prosperity gospel circles, and some Pentecostal preachers have accumulated massive amounts of wealth by collecting donations from their flocks. Their success is due in part to the fact that Pentecostal Christians really do believe that God wants everyone to enjoy the good things of life. Most Pentecostal churches advise members to avoid cheap and inappropriate pleasures because harm or sorrow often follow in their wake, but pleasure itself is not a problem, nor is wealth. In a Pentecostal view of the world, God wants people to flourish in every way possible, including financially. Greed is a sin, selfishness is a sin, and pride in one's wealth can be a sin, but being wealthy itself is not a sin and may in fact be a sign of favor from God.

It is important to remember the social context in which most of the world's Pentecostals live. More than 80 percent of the world's Pentecostal Christians live in Africa, Asia, and Latin America, and by almost any measure most of these individuals are decidedly poor. "Prosperity" for them does not mean two BMWs in the garage and a house at the beach. It means having enough food for today and possibly for tomorrow. It means having a roof that does not leak. It means obtaining a minimal level of education. It means having a job – any kind of job. When the prosperity gospel is promoted within a wealthy culture it can appear to be nothing more than religiously sanctioned greed, but in most worldwide contexts being wealthy means simply not worrying every day about meeting basic human needs for food, shelter, and safety. Most Pentecostals understand how easily prosperity preaching can go awry, but they also genuinely believe that God wants people to prosper. In their view, to squelch the preaching of prosperity would be to deny part of God's message of salvation.

If there is an Achilles' heel for the Pentecostal movement and its view of salvation, it is that all the grand promises of Christianity seem to hang by the very slender thread of human faith, and maintaining that faith – enough faith to believe in miracles – is a constant struggle in many Pentecostal circles. Lapses in belief or trust are sometimes seen as evidence that one is no longer Spirit-filled or even that one's salvation has been lost. Taken to the extreme, these concerns can result in an almost neurotic fixation on the current vitality of one's own faith: is my faith sufficiently fervent to guarantee salvation and God's continued blessing? For some, the pressure becomes simply too much, and many people have left the movement for that reason. Thus, alongside the ever-increasing numbers of Pentecostal Christians in the world, there is also a growing contingent of post-Pentecostal Christians who have exited the movement in search of a less pressure-packed form of faith.

Pentecostal History

It is difficult to decide where to begin the story of Pentecostalism. Something like Pentecostalism has appeared in flashes of Spirit-centered Christianity throughout Christian history. Speaking in tongues, healing the sick, performing miracles, having spiritual dreams and visions, and fighting off demons are common in various accounts from the Christian past. Many of these stories are inspiring. For example, the third-century martyr Perpetua had revelatory dreams that sustained her during her imprisonment before she was executed for her faith. The medieval Catholic philosopher Thomas Aquinas was so overwhelmed by powerful visions of heaven that he put down his pen and stopped writing at the end of his life. Francis Xavier, the sixteenth-century Jesuit missionary to Japan, was reportedly able to preach in Japanese without ever having been taught the language. But many pre-Pentecostal examples of Pentecostal-like faith are quite ordinary. Lots of Christians have hoped for healing, thought they heard God speaking to them, or experienced uncanny coincidences of need and assistance.

Examined with stories like these in mind, Pentecostalism can seem not at all novel. It can be construed as merely a continuation of the ways many Christians thought and acted before modern sensibilities made interacting with the supernatural seem strange and unusual. While there is a degree of plausibility in this interpretation, it does not seem sufficient to explain the rise and flourishing of contemporary Pentecostalism. Pentecostalism is not just a few individuals here and there who claim to have special encounters with the Holy Spirit. The Pentecostal movement is a huge global phenomenon involving more than half a billion people worldwide. Nothing similar has existed before. Pentecostalism obviously has some continuity with the Christian past – this is true of every Christian tradition – but it also represents an unprecedented break with the past. At no time in the past have so many Christians expected so much from God on an everyday basis. Pentecostalism is something new.

Modern Pentecostalism began in the early twentieth century when there was a sudden uptick in the number of Pentecost-like events taking place around the world. One incident happened at the Mukti Mission in Pune, India where Pandita Ramabai, an internationally known Hindu feminist convert to Christianity, led a Holy Spirit-filled revival at her school for girls during the years 1906 and 1907. Around the same time, the spiritual visionary Isaiah Shembe (1865–1935) began forming the new, independent *ama Nazaretha* church in South Africa that was both anticolonial and charismatic in orientation. Meanwhile, in Chile, the Methodist missionaries Willis and Mary Hoover began preaching about the gifts and power of the Holy Spirit, and their followers soon left the Methodist Church to start a new, independent Pentecostal church. Similar developments were also unfolding in Europe and North America, and participants began to wonder if God was launching a new spiritual initiative in the world.

In North America, Pentecostalism coalesced into a self-conscious movement around the year 1906 when a Spirit-centered revival exploded inside an old warehouse on Azusa Street, where a Black Holiness preacher named William J. Seymour was holding meetings. Seymour was an unassuming leader who sometimes eschewed preaching and sat in the front of the room praying silently – and yet the Spirit acted. People were slain in the Spirit, and they spoke in tongues. Just as miraculously, people of all races set their prejudices aside and embraced each other as equals. One observer remarked that the color line was washed away at Azusa, and Seymour himself always felt that love was the greatest miracle that occurred at the meetings. News of the revival spread quickly around the world. God seemed to be doing something new and special, raising up a "sign people"[5] from many different nations who exemplified both the universal love of God for all people and the wondrous power of the Holy Spirit in their lives. A second Pentecost was taking place.

One of the first reactions in religiously competitive North America was to organize, and a variety of Pentecostal denominations were created to fill the new Holy Spirit niche that had emerged in the country's spiritual marketplace. Organizers took cues from already existing churches when they explained the movement to their followers and to potential converts. The Assemblies of God, for example, adopted language from Reformed theology regarding sin, salvation, and the work of the Holy Spirit, which resulted in a two-step process where conversion is followed by baptism with the Holy Spirit. The Church of God (headquartered in Cleveland, Tennessee), by contrast, borrowed its theology from the Wesleyan Holiness movement, focusing on three stages of development in the Christian life: salvation followed by total sanctification which was the prerequisite for receiving the baptism with the Spirit. A group of "Jesus only" Pentecostals also took shape; they adopted a unitarian view of God that highlights the full and absolute divinity of Jesus who continues to be present in the world in the form of the Holy Spirit. As new organizations were built to house the movement, racial divisions also re-emerged. White Pentecostals abandoned their earlier alliances with Black Pentecostals, and churches were again divided along racial lines. As part of this process, the Church of God in Christ (COGIC), which had originally been an inclusive interracial church, became the largest of the predominantly African American Pentecostal denominations, and it remains so today.

Not everyone joined this institution-building frenzy. A number of prominent Pentecostal leaders chose to stay aloof and maintained their own independent Spirit-filled ministries, often as itinerant preachers and healers who wandered from place to place, addressing the needs of the sick and spreading the Pentecostal message wherever they went. Most of these independent preachers were less theologically dogmatic than their denominationalized peers, and they were willing to let God continue to surprise them. Kathryn Kuhlman sustained an independent Pentecostal ministry into the middle decades of the twentieth century, along with Oral Roberts (who founded a Pentecostal university) and many others. Their ministries nurtured a burgeoning interest in the work of the Holy Spirit from people who otherwise might never have heard the Pentecostal message.

The attention given to the Holy Spirit by people like Kuhlman and Roberts helped to launch the charismatic movement, which began around 1960. The charismatic movement is populated by people who are members of non-Pentecostal churches, but who see the miraculous work of the Holy Spirit as a normal part of their own Christian experience. These charismatic Christians have no intention of leaving their existing denominations to join an explicitly Pentecostal church. They are perfectly content to remain Baptists, Methodists, Presbyterians, or whatever, but their personal practice of faith has a distinctly Pentecostal flavor. By the late 1960s, not just Protestants but also some Catholics were joining the movement. Involvement in the Protestant wing of the charismatic movement peaked around 1990, and it has lost some vitality and visibility since then. By contrast, the Catholic charismatic movement (known as the Catholic Charismatic Renewal or just the CCR) has grown enormously and is still growing today.

Latin America has become the Charismatic Christian center of the world. Spirit-filled Christianity was first introduced to the region early in the twentieth century in the form of non-Catholic Pentecostalism. Pentecostalism grew relatively slowly during the first half of the century but then began to attract more converts, and the Catholic Church became worried. As one means of trying to stem the tide of converts away from Catholicism to Pentecostalism, many bishops began promoting the CCR as a Catholic alternative for people interested in a Pentecostal-like faith. Since then, the CCR in Latin America has exploded in size, with the largest gains in Brazil, where the singing padre Marcelo Rossi, a former aerobics instructor who is now a Catholic priest, has been the most prominent CCR leader. Roughly a quarter of the region's Catholics have adopted a Charismatic orientation, a higher percentage of Charismatic Christians than anywhere else in the world. Non-Catholic Pentecostalism has also flourished in Latin America, and it currently accounts for about 15 percent of the Christian population in the region.

Pentecostal growth has been similarly robust in twentieth-century Africa, but the dynamics are more complex. The foundational layer of Pentecostalism in Africa is comprised of the various Independent or African Initiated Churches (AICs) that formed during the late nineteenth and early twentieth centuries. One example of an AIC is the Kimbanguist Church which began in the 1920s. Simon Kimbangu was a Baptist catechist helping missionaries do their work when God spoke to him in a dream and called him to be an apostle and to start his own new church. At first, Kimbangu hesitated, but he was eventually convinced by God to step out in faith and to create a new Christian movement where all the miraculous gifts of the Holy Spirit were respected, including speaking in unknown tongues. Kimbangu's reputation as a healer and spiritual visionary quickly spread throughout the Congo, which worried the local Belgian colonial authorities. He was arrested in 1921 and kept in prison until he died in 1951, but his church – the Church of Jesus Christ on Earth by His Special Envoy Simon Kimbangu – survived, and it still has millions of members today. Kimbangu never called himself Pentecostal, but his church, and hundreds of similarly Spirit-centered AICs that emerged during the last century, proclaim a message and way of faith that is essentially Pentecostal in content and emphases.

In the years following World War II, a more traditionally denominational variety of Pentecostalism began to appear. Nigeria has been at the forefront of this development, and about a third of all Nigerian Christians are now Pentecostal. The Redeemed Christian Church of God (RCCG), founded in 1952 and currently led by the Rev. Enoch Adeboye, attracts 50,000 worshippers to the home congregation in Lagos each week, and the denomination's annual gathering, called Redemption Camp, draws in excess of two million people. The RCCG has more than 10,000 congregations worldwide, located in 120 nations. Other Nigerian Pentecostal churches, including the Living Faith Church (also known as the Winners Chapel), The Lord's Chosen, and Word of Life Bible Church, have also become huge international ecclesiastical conglomerates. All of these churches preach a message of spiritual protection, deliverance, prosperity, and empowerment that has proven appeal in Africa. It is a message that is increasingly popular any place where poor but optimistic Christians are looking for churches that will support them and their dreams for a better life.

What makes the situation in Africa unique is the ubiquity of Pentecostal beliefs and attitudes across African Christianity as a whole. An estimated 80 percent of all African Christians believe in miracles; 50 to 60 percent believe that God will reward people with prosperity if they have enough faith to claim it; more than half believe they are living in the end times and Jesus will return to earth during their lifetime; and nearly 50 percent believe they need protection from witches and evil spirits.[6] All of these beliefs are functionally Pentecostal, but they are affirmed by millions of African Anglicans, Baptists, Lutherans, Methodists, Mennonites, Presbyterians, and others. Are these individuals Protestants or Pentecostals? One way of answering that question is to observe what happens when these individuals migrate elsewhere, especially to North America or Europe. Very often, these African Christians end up joining a Pentecostal church in their new locations, because Pentecostal churches feel so much more like home than the non-African versions of their African Protestant denominations. Large swaths of the Christian churches in Africa have become functionally Pentecostal even though most members of those churches would deny being Pentecostal.

The ambiguities of Pentecostal identity in Africa – the fuzzy border lines of the movement – are also an issue in North America. In the 1980s and 1990s some Pentecostal churches began downplaying their distinctively Pentecostal practices (like speaking in tongues and public prophesying) after several highly visible Pentecostal television preachers were involved in embarrassing sex scandals. Simultaneously, many evangelical Protestant churches became more emotionally expressive and adopted Pentecostal-like worship practices such as singing praise songs with hands raised in the air. Several new denominations, like Calvary Chapel (headquartered in Costa Mesa, California), stepped into the gap by developing statements of faith that intentionally smudged the differences between moderate Pentecostalism and emotionally oriented evangelical Protestantism. It is now sometimes difficult to distinguish toned-down Pentecostalism from Spirit-sensitive evangelicalism in North America, and this same phenomenon is also evident in East Asia.

Institutional and Social Structure of Pentecostalism

In the Gospel of John, the Holy Spirit is likened to the wind that blows wherever it wants without warning or predictability, and Pentecostal Christians perceive their work in the same way. They may sometimes plan and plant new churches in good institutional fashion, but they are always on the lookout for places where God's Spirit may unexpectedly be blowing, and they want to be ready to follow. This attitude provides considerable leeway to entrepreneurial leaders who are self-starting and innovative, which is one reason why the movement has grown so quickly: someone has always been there to step up to meet every perceived need. But entrepreneurial leaders also tend to have enormous egos, and this too has been characteristic of Pentecostalism. The resultant social terrain of the Pentecostal movement is uneven and somewhat chaotic. Certain zones of Pentecostal activity are highly organized and tightly controlled. This is the case, for example, with the Assemblies of God, a well-oiled Pentecostal denomination (which prefers to be called a "fellowship") that keeps close watch on its pastors and its congregations and tries quickly to suppress any divergence from approved standards. Other Pentecostal associations and congregations are much more relaxed and freewheeling.

Pentecostalism as a movement has no central authority and its edges are remarkably indistinct, but nonetheless there is a strong sense of Pentecostal identity and mutual responsibility. Pentecostals care about what other Pentecostals are doing, regardless of denominational affiliation or location. They look out for each other, and they also keep an eye on each other. They know that the reputation of Pentecostalism in its entirety can be affected by the misdeeds of anyone. Pentecostalism is still largely an oral tradition that operates by word of mouth, and if any one group or leader gets noticeably out of line others will hear about it and intervene if the misdeeds seem sufficiently egregious. Such interventions are not always successful, but they carry weight because no one wants to lose their reputation in a movement where word-of-mouth reputation is precisely what conveys status and influence. (Protestantism has similar but weaker tradition-wide checks and balances, while Catholicism and Orthodoxy typically handle accusations regarding clerical or institutional misdeeds through well-established official processes.)

The social structure of Pentecostalism as a whole can be pictured as three concentric circles (see Figure 5.2) with an inner core consisting of all the many different churches, denominations, associations, and organizations that are distinctively and unapologetically Pentecostal in their practices and beliefs. This core includes Pentecostal denominations like the Assemblies of God and the Redeemed Christian Church of God; it includes most of the independent indigenous churches in Africa and elsewhere; it includes single-congregation Pentecostal churches like the huge Yoido Full Gospel Church in Seoul, South Korea; and it includes recently organized, moderately Pentecostal groups like Calvary Chapel. The second circle represents the charismatic movement, and it is composed of individuals who personally embrace Pentecostal ideas and practices but who remain members of various non-Pentecostal churches, including the Catholic Church. The third, fuzzily bounded outer circle represents Pentecostalism's larger zone of influence that extends to churches and individuals that are not Pentecostal themselves but that have become more attuned to the ongoing work of the Holy Spirit. This third circle can be called the Pentecostal *penumbra*, and it includes everyone who has, consciously or unconsciously, added some Pentecostal characteristics and sensibilities to their practice of Christian faith. Many evangelical Protestants and most African Christians now exemplify this dynamic.

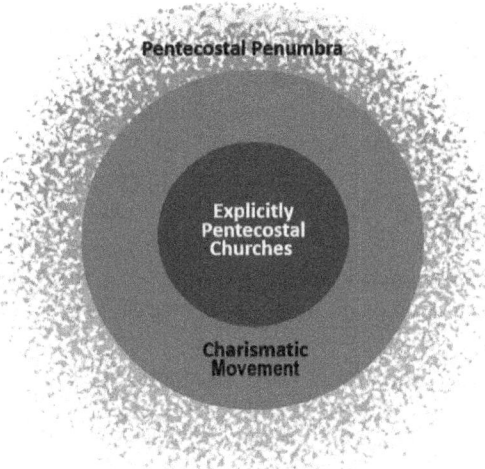

Figure 5.2 Social structure of Pentecostalism.

To some extent, every Christian tradition can be diagramed in this same way. Every Christian tradition has its core membership, plus various groups of people who self-consciously participate in the tradition without becoming formal members, and then a wider circle of individuals who may be attracted to certain aspects of the tradition but who do not consider themselves to be part of the tradition. But Pentecostalism differs from other Christian traditions in both the size and composition of these circles. There are 300 million Christians or more who belong to explicitly Pentecostal churches worldwide, another 200 million people or more are involved in the charismatic movement, and an additional 200 to 300 million Christians around the globe easily qualify as part of the Pentecostal penumbra. No other Christian tradition has spread its influence so widely; Pentecostalism can slip and slide into places where other traditions cannot. Orthodoxy and Catholicism are almost entirely contained within their formal church structures, and Protestantism resides mainly in the many differently shaped church and parachurch institutions and organizations it has produced. Pentecostalism, by contrast, is held in leaky institutional buckets. The tradition frequently seeps out and soaks the social ground around it – and most Pentecostal Christians are not at all concerned about that leakage. After all, the goal of the Pentecostal movement is not to harness or control the power of the Spirit; instead, its goal is to help all people to open their hearts and lives to God's unexpected presence and unpredictable actions in the world

Notes

1 *Los Angeles Times* (April 18, 1906), p. 1.
2 William H. Durham, "Personal Testimony of Pastor Durham," *Pentecostal Testimony*, 1:3 (undated but likely 1909), p. 7.
3 D. Wesley Myland, *The Latter Rain Covenant and Pentecostal Power with Testimony of Healings and Baptism* (Chicago, IL: Evangel Publishing House, 1910), pp. 25–26.
4 Kathryn Kuhlman, *I Believe in Miracles* (Alachua, FL: Bridge-Logos, 2006), p. 4.
5 Elizabeth Sisson, *A Sign People* (Springfield, MO: Gospel Publishing House, 1918).
6 See *Tolerance and Tension: Islam and Christianity in Sub-Saharan Africa*, Pew Forum on Religion and Public Life (April 2010), https://www.pewforum.org/2010/04/15/executive-summary-islam-and-christianity-in-sub-saharan-africa (accessed May 29, 2020).

6

Becoming Global

Christianity's different traditions play a huge role in shaping how Christians experience and express their faith, but those traditions have themselves been deeply influenced by the cultural and geographic locations where they began, developed, and were later exported. The importance of these cultural and geographic factors has become ever more evident in recent decades as Christianity has spread around the globe. It is no longer adequate to answer the question "What is Christianity?" by referencing the movement's major traditions alone. Place and culture must also be taken into account. This chapter provides a broad-brush portrait of Christianity's transformation from a predominantly European movement to becoming a genuinely global religion.

Christianity originally began in the Middle East and then expanded widely to both East and West. By the year 700, Christianity had established its presence in a huge territory that ranged across more than 5000 miles, from Ireland in the West to China in the East. That was the highwater mark, and then the geographic scope of Christianity began to contract. In Asia, where Christianity had never become the majority religion, it slowly withered under intensifying levels of persecution. Meanwhile, the Christian population of Europe grew exponentially and also became wealthier and more powerful. By the year 1500, Christianity had become an almost exclusively European religion. But then Europeans themselves started re-exporting Christianity around the world, and today Christianity is once again a global faith. The re-globalization of Christianity took centuries to complete, and initially the growth of Christianity outside of Europe was so slow that it was almost statistically invisible. But then, in the twentieth century, the dam broke. By 1950, the European share of the world Christian population had fallen below 50 percent for the first time in a millennium. Today, three-quarters of the world's Christians are non-European (see Figure 6.1).

Christians now live in every nation on earth, and this global expansion of Christianity did not happen accidently. Christians intentionally, and sometimes aggressively, spread their message around the world, and many different non-European people eventually embraced it. Catholics were the first to engage in

What Is Christianity? First Edition. Douglas Jacobsen.
© 2022 John Wiley & Sons Ltd. Published 2022 by John Wiley & Sons Ltd.

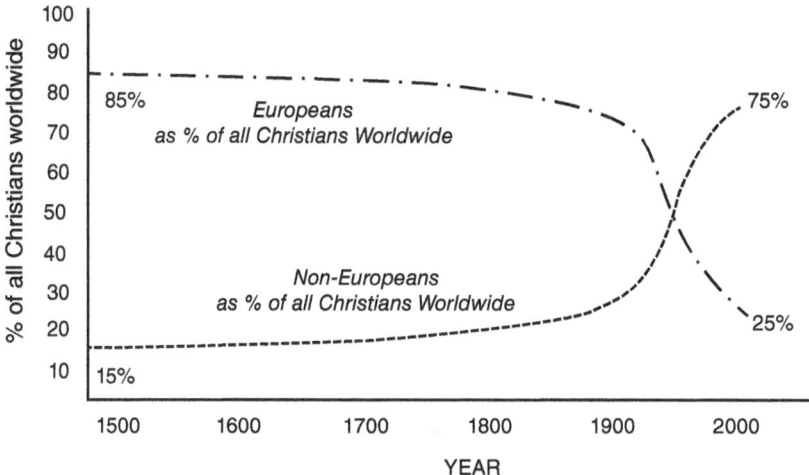

Figure 6.1 Graph showing changing percentage of all Christians who lived in Europe and who lived elsewhere during the period 1500 to the present.

this work, but Protestants eventually joined enthusiastically and in recent decades so have Pentecostals. Orthodox Christians, by contrast, were historically much less involved in global Christian missions, largely because they were struggling to survive under Muslim rule or lived in countries that lacked the resources needed to support overseas missions. Consequently, Orthodox Christianity has experienced a relative decline in global size and influence compared to the other three major Christian traditions.

The stories of individual missionaries who spent their lives trying to convert the world to faith in Christ are often quite inspiring. They left friends and family behind and headed off to unknown lands to tell people about Jesus. But simultaneously, and whether they were consciously aware of it or not, these missionaries were also actors in Europe's colonization of the world, and that colonization was often brutal. In many regions of the world, Christianity was introduced to the local population through an awkward mixture of conquest and compassion, and both missionaries and local converts had to sort through that mix trying to discern which elements were good and helpful and which were evil and destructive. Christianity itself was re-imagined in the process.

Catholic Globalization

Catholics were the first Europeans to intentionally export their faith around the globe. While some forays into Asia had taken place earlier, this work began in earnest during the late 1400s, when Portugal began poking its way down the west coast of Africa, exploring the region, acquiring slaves, and seeking converts. Shortly thereafter, the newly wedded Catholic monarchs of Spain, Ferdinand and Isabella, also joined in this effort, sending out soldiers, explorers, and priests to conquer the world and Christianize its inhabitants. To aid in this work, the pope gave the Spanish and Portuguese monarchs (and their royal heirs) extraordinary permission to organize and oversee the Catholic Church in any lands they conquered. This meant there was literally no daylight between the church and the state in the emerging Spanish and Portuguese empires, and this merger of faith and governmental power deeply shaped local perceptions of Christianity.

Spain focused its efforts on the Americas, and soldiers led the way. The conquistadores believed that conquest needed to precede evangelism, and they told the region's inhabitants that their options were either to submit to God and the Spanish monarchy or to be attacked, raped, enslaved, and subjected to "all the mischief and damage" the Spanish soldiers could muster.[1] This warning was usually issued in a language that the local people could not understand, but any confusion or hesitation was read as resistance, so violence was the typical response. One Spanish theologian provided the horrifying rationale that "terror" was often very effective in dispelling error and in spreading "the light of truth" among "heathen" people.[2] Indigenous warriors were killed, indigenous women were violently assaulted, and thousands of indigenous people were enslaved and put to work serving the needs and desires of their conquerors. In exchange, Spanish colonists gave the indigenous people an opportunity to save their own souls by embracing European Catholicism.

A tiny handful of Catholic leaders protested the violence of the conquest and the ensuing oppression of the people. Perhaps most famously, the Dominican friar Antonio de Montesinos preached a sermon to his Spanish colonial parish members on Christmas Eve in 1511, informing them that they were living in mortal sin "by reason of the cruelty and tyranny that you practice on these innocent people." He then rebuked them:

> Tell me, by what right or justice do you hold these Indians in such cruel and horrible slavery? By what right do you wage such detestable wars on these people who lived mildly and peacefully in their own lands, where you have consumed infinite numbers of them with unheard of murders and desolations?...Are they not men? Do they not have rational souls? Are you not bound to love them as you love yourselves? How can you lie in such profound and lethargic slumber? Be sure that in your present state you can no more be saved than the Moors or Turks who do not have and do not want the faith of Jesus Christ.[3]

Despite the friar's warning, the abuse continued. Some indigenous people were worked to death; many more died from the importation of European diseases against which the indigenous people had no immunity. As the local population dwindled, enslaved African people were imported to replenish the labor force, which layered injustice upon injustice. Today less than 10 percent of the Latin American population is indigenous, but *mestizos* (people of mixed indigenous and European ancestry) comprise close to half the population. There is also a large African-descended population, especially in the Caribbean and Brazil where roughly 80 percent of the Africans brought to the Americas were enslaved.

This swirl of violence and oppression defined the context in which the message of Christ was first introduced to Latin America, which made it nearly impossible for the indigenous people to respond positively to the gospel message. For them, the Christian God was a powerful and violent deity who could not be defeated, so they submitted to the Spanish conquistadores and to their religion because they had no other choice. They became Christians in name, but not, at least initially, in heart. Problems were exacerbated by the fact that baptism was often administered before any meaningful instruction about Christian faith had been offered. Declared to be Christians, the indigenous people were then largely left to sort out the implications of their new religion for themselves. Missionary priests tried to assist, but the task was immense. Not surprisingly, the self-constructed faith of the local people often did not align with the official teachings of Catholicism.

What made the difference in Latin America, what finally helped the people of the region to look beyond the violence of the conquest and to see Christ as a merciful savior, was the Virgin Mary. In 1531, Mary, appearing as the Virgin of Guadalupe, spoke to a *mestizo* peasant named Cuauhtlatoatzin – his baptismal name was Juan Diego – on a hill in what is now part of Mexico City. She told Cuauhtlatoatzin that she (and, by implication, her son Jesus and God, his father) loved and cared for *all* the people of the earth. At first this was hard to believe. The European God that the Spanish conquest had introduced to the region seemed drenched with blood and filled with hatred for all non-Europeans. But the Mary who spoke to Cuauhtlatoatzin was not European; she looked and spoke like an indigenous woman, and so he listened and he took the Virgin's words to heart. Many other Latin American Catholics have followed that same path, heeding the message of God's love as expressed by the Virgin of Guadalupe and by Mary in other representations throughout the region. To this day, Mary is uniquely honored by Latin American Catholics as the one who revealed God's true nature and enabled them to embrace the gospel joyfully as the good news it was meant to be, and Cuauhtlatoatzin is now officially recognized as a Catholic saint.

About the same time that Spain was invading the Americas, Portuguese explorers were arriving in India. Vasco de Gama was the commander in charge, who sailed into the southern port city of Calicut in 1498 and said he was looking for spices and Christians. The logic behind his search for spices is self-evident; his quest to find Christians was rooted in a medieval myth about a Christian kingdom hidden somewhere in Asia. European Christians had long harbored hope for discovering this kingdom so that Christians from East and West could join forces for a coordinated two-front attack on Muslims in the Middle East.

The Portuguese were initially delighted to find Christians in India, and these were practicing Christians who claimed roots that extended all the way back to St. Thomas the apostle in the first century. However, Portuguese attitudes changed dramatically once they learned more about them. Indian Christians were associated with the ancient Church of the East, and their religious practices and ideas did not align neatly with European Catholicism. This was deemed to be thoroughly unacceptable, so the militarily superior Portuguese launched a violent inquisition against the local Indian Christian community to force conformity to European-style Catholicism. Their efforts culminated in 1599 with the Synod of Diamper, which condemned many local Christian practices for being too culturally Indian and banned most books and other writings produced by the Indian church. Massive piles of Indian Christian literature and church records were burned in an effort to destroy all memory of India's non-Catholic Christian past, and the local Christian population was forced to become Catholic. In subsequent centuries, some Indian Christians continued to affiliate with the Catholic Church, but many others left the Catholic Church as soon as it was safe to do so and tried to resuscitate their own distinctively Indian Christian faith.

Catholic missionaries took a more hospitable approach in just a few places, almost always in locations where European military assistance was lacking so that missionaries had to rely on persuasion alone in their evangelistic efforts. The premier example is provided by the Jesuits in China. Rather than condemning Chinese culture, the Jesuits tried to build bridges of understanding between Christianity and Chinese ways of thought and life, and they even allowed Chinese converts to continue participating in some local cultural rituals (which were difficult to distinguish from religious rites). Because of their respect for Chinese culture and their courteous approach to conversion, Jesuit missionaries were welcomed into the country and were officially allowed to pursue their work.

However, the Jesuit's non-aggressive style of evangelism was not appreciated by other Catholic missionaries in the region, who wrote to the Vatican expressing their criticism of what they saw as the Jesuit's improper and possibly heretical approach. Pope Clement XI (in office from 1700 to 1721) immediately sided with the Jesuits' critics; he condemned the Jesuit policy and declared that there should be no religious accommodations for local cultural practices. This fracas came to be known as the Chinese Rites Controversy, and the pope's stance was clear: only European-style Catholicism was true Catholicism and any attempt to Asianize the faith was forbidden. In response to the pope's condemnation of the Jesuits, the Chinese Emperor Kangxi banned all Catholic missionaries from his territories and declared that Catholicism had shown itself to be no different from any other inconsequential and bigoted religious sect.

In the centuries since the Chinese Rites Controversy, Catholic missionary efforts around the world have come to rely more and more on persuasion rather than on threats or coercion, and this change was hastened by the decline of the Spanish and Portuguese empires. While Catholic evangelism became kinder, many Catholic leaders continued to believe that European Catholicism was the rightful standard for Catholicism everywhere. Pope Clement XI's anti-accommodationist missionary policy was not formally reversed until the mid-twentieth century, and as late as the year 2000 (in a document entitled *Dominus Iesus*) the Vatican expressed concern that some Asian Catholic bishops were being too accommodating of Asian values and ideas. In 2006, Pope Benedict XVI declared that Christianity, "despite its origins and some significant developments in the East, finally took on its historically decisive character in Europe."[4] For Pope Benedict, Catholicism's acquired Europeanness is not accidental or peripheral. It is ordained by God, and it is intended to be permanent. People from other parts of the world may decorate their Catholicism around the edges with their own local customs, but the core of Catholic teaching, according to Pope Benedict, is indissolubly linked to European modes of thought and rationality, and this European Catholic core is not open to modification.

These comments by Pope Benedict were not delivered *ex cathedra* so they are not binding on all Catholics, but the simple fact that a German-born pope felt compelled to reaffirm Catholicism's Europeanness signals a change in Catholic realities. Few Catholics any longer think of Europe as the moral and spiritual heartland of Catholicism, and most Catholic missionaries now think their work properly involves the inculturation (or indigenization) of the gospel in the different cultures where they serve. The goal of missions is explicitly not to reproduce European Catholicism elsewhere, but instead to allow local Catholics to adapt the faith, as needed and appropriate, to local circumstances. If any place in the world has become the new heartland of Catholicism, it is Latin America, where 40 percent of the world's Catholics now live. This historic shift is personified by the selection of Jorge Mario Bergoglio, the former Archbishop of Buenos Aires, Argentina, to become the first non-European-born pope in many centuries, and as Pope Francis he is helping to move the Catholic tradition as a whole beyond its historic Eurocentrism.

Protestant Globalization

Protestant missionary efforts around the globe began much later than Catholic endeavors. The Protestant movement itself did not begin until the early 1500s, and initially all energy was directed toward securing a safe presence in Europe. But even after Protestantism was well established, missionary efforts lagged. One reason for this slow start was that there was no predominantly Protestant nation that could rival the colonial power of Spain or Portugal. So, Protestantism's early efforts outside of Europe were cautious and piecemeal.

The first Protestant expansion outside of Europe took place in North America, but this initiative was not, for the most part, mission driven. Instead, Protestants were seeking their own economic advancement and religious freedom, which in this case meant freedom from persecution at the hands of other Protestants. Many of the Protestants who headed for North America were Puritans who believed that the Church of England was insufficiently Protestant and who had been trying to make the English church more Protestant. They had raised the ire of Queen Elizabeth and her successors King James I and King Charles I, who decided to squelch the Puritan movement, and emigration was one way of avoiding their wrath. In a sense, leaving for North America was an admission of defeat, but settling in "new" England also provided Puritans with a fresh start and a way to prove that ultimately God was on their side.

North America was not empty land, and Protestant settlers had to make judgments about their relationship to the Native American population. Some Protestants initially suggested that Native Americans might have been unaffected by the Fall and were still living in an Edenic state of innocence before God and each other, but this relatively positive assessment soon gave way to negative stereotyping of Native Americans as lazy. Since the indigenous people were not *improving* the land – since they were not farming it, mining it, or grazing it – the new settlers claimed both a right and an obligation to seize the land and put it to good use. Protestant settlers never enslaved the native people of North America, not because they were opposed to slavery (many of them participated enthusiastically in the transatlantic slave trade), but because of their assumption that Native Americans were too indolent to become good workers. When infectious diseases imported from Europe ravaged the native population in North America with the same ruthless efficiency that had depleted the indigenous population in Latin America, many settlers interpreted this catastrophe as a "wonder-working providence."[5] God was miraculously emptying the land of its previous inhabitants so that European Protestants could settle there.

European diseases did not obliterate all Native American communities, and before long North American Protestants were pushing, shoving, and fighting their way across the continent, driving any remaining Native Americans further and further west away from their ancestral territories. Protestant North Americans eventually came to believe it was their "manifest destiny" to control the entirety of North America, that God intended them to subdue the continent and, in their eyes, to save the region from both Indian savagery and Catholic domination. The final push to the Pacific Ocean required defeating not only Native American communities but also well-established Spanish-speaking, Catholic settlements in the southwest and along the coast of California. Christian moral codes imposed few checks on the violence, and the mission was accomplished. North America has been predominantly Protestant ever since, an outcome that resulted almost entirely from aggressive immigration, not from conversion of the indigenous population.

While a few intrepid Protestants had begun spreading Christianity outside of Europe (and outside of North America) in the early 1700s, Protestant global missions did not begin in earnest until the late 1700s. One of the first countries to be targeted was India, and the primary focus of this missionary venture was educational because true conversion requires informed assent. The initial step was accordingly to become familiar with Indian culture and translate the Bible into languages that local people could understand. Indians were then enrolled in literacy classes so they could learn how to read the Bible and acquire the full capacity to accept or reject the gospel for themselves.

These early Protestant missionaries quickly discovered, however, that Indian society was more complex than they had anticipated, and conversion involved more than merely accepting or rejecting the message of the Bible. Which parts of Indian culture could be affirmed and used to explain the gospel, and which parts should be denounced as evil? Should the caste system be criticized, or should it simply be accepted as part of the Indian way of life? Should Christians condemn social practices like *sati* (the ritual immolation of widows) or should they proceed without comment? And what strategy of evangelism should they pursue? Should they try to convert the Hindu elite first, so that everyone else would then follow, or should they direct their initial efforts toward India's sub-caste (Dalit) population because they were most oppressed? None of these questions had easy answers, and Protestant missionaries, following in the footsteps of their Catholic counterparts, began to realize how intellectually and morally difficult the work of evangelism can be.

As the nineteenth century progressed, Protestant missionary activity became increasingly intertwined with British imperialism. Following the collapse of the Spanish and Portuguese empires, Great Britain became the world's leading colonial power. Protestant missionaries were never as closely connected to the colonial enterprise as the Catholic Church had been in Latin America, but Protestant missions often were located where colonial amenities were available, and their evangelistic efforts utilized the colonial infrastructure (such as roads, mail service, and the justice system). Perhaps most crucially, British colonizers and Protestant missionaries shared the same basic attitude toward the colonized population, an attitude that mixed paternalism with racism and that paired altruism with self-confident arrogance. The British writer and colonial cheerleader Rudyard Kipling composed a poem entitled "The White Man's Burden" that implored Protestants to "send forth the best ye breed...to serve their captives' need," and he described these captives as both "wild" and "half devil and half child."[6] British colonialists and Protestant missionaries shared the goal of saving and civilizing these supposedly "wild" human beings, and the difference between their two concerns, the distinction between salvation and civilization, was often hard to discern.

Within the context of colonialism, the dynamics of conversion were rarely straightforward for converts themselves. Many new Protestant converts in Africa and Asia (Latin America was largely ignored because it was already solidly Catholic) were surely attracted to Christianity for genuinely spiritual reasons, but conversion was also a pathway to social and financial advancement within the colonial system. Potential converts were aware that becoming a Christian might be the only way to gain admission to a desirable school, and some individuals converted because they were social outcasts in their own communities and conversion was a chance for a new life. While conversion to Christianity clearly had a religious dimension, conversion in a colonial context inevitably involved a host of other social and psychological considerations as well.

Whatever the pathway to conversion, it would have been nearly impossible for any person from Africa or Asia to embrace Protestantism in the precise form that most missionaries thought they were preaching it. European and American missionaries rarely mastered all the languages in the local regions where they served, so they often communicated in the local pidgin (colonial trade language), which usually had a limited vocabulary and was not designed for discussing the intricacies of faith and spirituality. In addition, missionaries typically relied on catechists (indigenous lay preachers) to help spread their message. Missionaries were inclined to view these catechists as mere translators, but there is no such thing as the *mere* translation of religious ideas and practices. Translation always involves some (re)interpretation, so the Protestant faith that was embraced by African and Asian converts was almost always an already partially indigenized version of Christianity, which was then further adapted to local circumstances by individual converts and their communities.

At times, the results were dramatic. Protestantism encourages believers to think for themselves, and the thinking of some converts was so creative that the end result was hardly recognizable as Christianity. One of the most extreme examples occurred in mid-nineteenth century China when a convert named Hong Xiuquan (1814–1864) had a revelatory dream telling him that he was the younger brother of Jesus. As the Asian son of God, Hong said he had been commanded to establish a divine kingdom of *taiping* (peace and security) in China. His new version of Christianity attracted millions of armed followers, and by the time the Chinese central government finally defeated the Taiping Rebellion more than 20 million people had died in the bloodiest civil war in all of human history. Ever since, Chinese governments have been leery of Christianity (and of religion in general), and Protestant missionaries have been keenly aware of how dangerous unrestrained indigenization can be.

Despite such worries, Protestant missionaries were often unable to prevent converts from launching their own new indigenously controlled churches in Africa and Asia. This is, after all, precisely what Protestants are supposed to do: they are supposed to read the Bible for themselves and then try to live according to what they have learned – and when they learned that missionaries had gotten some things wrong (or perhaps had lied about what the Bible really said), they would launch their own new churches in an effort to be more faithful to what God desired.

Africa was especially fertile soil for independent, indigenous Protestantism, and during the last century thousands of new African Initiated Churches (AICs) have sprung up in sub-Saharan Africa. Created by African Christians for African Christians and organized in thoroughly African fashion, these churches are totally independent of Western control or guidance. Many of these new churches were prompted by specific flashpoints of difference. Western missionaries to Africa were apt to teach that polygamy was wrong, that dreams signified nothing, and that miracles were rare, but upon reading the Bible for themselves local converts discovered a world where God did not unambiguously condemn polygamy, where God often spoke to people through dreams, and where miracles happened all the time. Many AICs were established in response to these divergences and, not surprisingly, their spiritual preferences often tilted toward Pentecostalism, rather than toward traditional Protestantism.

Until the middle of the twentieth century, many Protestant missionaries vigorously condemned these AICs, but in subsequent decades most missionaries began viewing themselves as colleagues and co-workers with African Independent Christians and with other African or Asian Christians who wanted to indigenize their faith. This change in attitudes did not come easily since many Protestant missionaries worried that indigenization would open the door to syncretism (the indiscriminate mixing of religious ideas) and heresy, but most of them ultimately concluded that God was somehow active in the midst of all this religious creativity, and they did not want to get in God's way. Like their Catholic counterparts, the great majority of Protestant missionaries today perceive their role as one of assisting other Christians around the world, not as being in charge.

The Bigger Picture: From Eurocentrism to World Christianity

Over the course of the twentieth century, Christianity grew beyond its Eurocentric orientation and became a genuinely global religion. This transition was partly the result of missionary efforts, but it might never have happened, or it certainly would not have happened as quickly, if changes in the global geo-political landscape had not forced Christians to change their perceptions of the world and themselves. At the beginning of the twentieth century, Christians in Europe and North America were still hugely optimistic about where the world was headed. In their eyes, Western culture seemed to epitomize the hopes and dreams of humanity; they thought their own civilization, including Christianity, represented what everyone else instinctively wanted. What's more, the whole world seemed to be slowly turning their way. European culture in general and Christianity in particular seemed to be flourishing everywhere. John R. Mott, general secretary of the YMCA in the United States and Canada, gave voice to these sentiments in his book *The Evangelization of the World in This Generation*, which was published in 1901. Never before in all of history, he noted, had Christians been more "united in the sublime purpose of enthroning Jesus Christ as King among all nations and races of men."[7] He expected that very soon, in his own lifetime, the whole world would become Christian, and it would become Christian in the Western ways that Mott and his contemporaries, whether Protestant or Catholic, thought were best.

This almost giddy confidence in Western culture and Christianity ended abruptly with the outbreak of World War I (1914–1918), which was known at the time as the Great War. Sparked by a combination of secret treaties and nationalistic hubris, and fueled by everyone's unthinking assumption that God was obviously on their side, Europeans rushed into one of the most bitter and irrational wars ever fought. Christians killed Christians with reckless abandon. The idea of inevitable progress died on the muddy battlefields along with 10 million soldiers and another 10 million civilians. Optimism lingered a bit longer in the United States, where people thought they were fighting a "war to make the world safe for democracy" and where casualties were relatively low, but the Great Depression (1929–1939) eventually deflated American optimism, too.

The West's missionary efforts continued despite the difficulties of the time, but spirits were subdued and fewer people were available to do the work. When World War II began in September 1939, everything was put on hold once again. Many missionaries were called home, and Europe's colonial governments were stretched thin. The war lasted for six long years, and it was the bloodiest war in human history. More than 50 million people died worldwide. Russia and China suffered the most deaths by far, but almost every nation in the world was profoundly affected. This time, no one saw the war as a religious crusade. The far greater peril was religious inaction. As Germany rounded up Jews throughout Europe and sent them to death camps, very few Christians raised their voices in protest. A small handful of Christians in Germany and in German-occupied lands took a public stand against Nazism, and a few brave souls hid Jews in their homes, but most Christians remained silent and some actively cheered for the Nazis.

After the War, German Protestant churches offered a weak apology for the wrongs that had been perpetrated by their country, but they failed to mention the Holocaust specifically. As for the Catholic Church, scholars are still debating whether the pope was complicit in the Holocaust or if, instead, he tried to limit its worst horrors. In 1998, the Catholic Church finally apologized for failing to explicitly challenge the Holocaust while it was underway. Neither Protestants nor Catholics have fully acknowledged the degree to which Christianity itself supplied the religious fuel that fed the fires of antisemitism and paved the road to genocide.

All of Europe's churches were morally diminished by the two world wars, and some Europeans began looking elsewhere for sources of moral guidance, social cohesion, and public values. In Western Europe, religion seemed increasingly irrelevant to the needs of the time, and people began to simply ignore it. Eastern Europe faced a far more difficult situation. Communists took control of Russia in 1917, and following World War II they extended their rule over all of Eastern Europe. Christians suffered terribly as Communist governments tried to suppress or entirely eradicate religion. Communism was also adopted in China and later in Cuba, and Christians worldwide reacted with alarm. Instead of feeling as if they were poised to celebrate the enthronement of Jesus Christ as King, Christians suddenly felt under attack. Their previous plans about Christianizing and civilizing the globe's non-Christian people gave way to the urgent new goal of Christianizing the world in order to stop the Communist menace. The United States, which had emerged from World War II as the world's first superpower, took the lead in this new quasi-religious Cold War against Communism, and American Christians were quite confident that they would prevail.

That was the view from the Global North, but Christians (and others) in the Global South had a far different perspective regarding the shifting dynamics of global political power. At the beginning of the twentieth century, Christian Europe ruled almost half the world through its colonial system and, at the conclusion of World War II, most of that colonial system remained fully intact. It was only in the postwar years that the European powers finally, grudgingly loosened their grip on their colonial possessions. The Middle East (Jordan, Syria, and Lebanon) broke free first, in 1946, along with the Philippines. British rule in India and Pakistan ended in 1947. Independence was delayed in Southeast Asia, and the process was bloodier. In Indonesia, 300,000 people died in battle before the Dutch finally relinquished their claims on the country in 1949, and an estimated three million people were killed in Vietnam, first at the hands of the French and later the United States, before full independence was achieved in 1973. In Africa, the dismantling of colonialism began in the 1960s and took more than two decades to complete. As in Asia, the process was often bitter and bloody.

The protracted process of decolonization and the vehemence with which Europe's colonizing nations tried to hold on to their power convinced much of the world that the West was not to be trusted. In 1955, delegates from a group of non-Western nations, representing more than half the population of the planet, gathered in Bandung, Indonesia to discuss their shared future. They were not as much concerned about Communism as they were about colonial oppression and the neocolonial arrangements of indirect economic control that often followed. They were also explicitly concerned about the role of race in world affairs. Why, they wondered, were the darker skinned people of the world always ruled by lighter skinned people? Wasn't it time for this to change? Wasn't it time for the "colored peoples"[8] of the world, as President Sukarno of Indonesia described the meeting's participants, to claim their adulthood and take back control of their nations from the white Christian countries of the West who had dominated them for so long?

The Bandung meeting was a gathering of politicians, not Christians, but many Christians from Africa, Asia, and Latin America shared Sukarno's sentiments. They felt it was time to take control of their own lives and churches and to free themselves from the paternalistic supervision of Western Christians. This was not at all a rejection of Christianity itself; it was only a rejection of Western dominance. In 1971 a group of leaders from a number of African Protestant churches called for a moratorium on Western missionary activity, because they no longer wanted or needed any Christian guidance or tutoring from the West. A total moratorium was never achieved, but the signal had been given for creating a new, solidly African Christianity.

A few years later, in 1975, Edward Fasholé-Luke, an Anglican theologian from Sierra Leone, articulated a new rule of thumb for African Christianity: in order to be genuinely Christian, African Christianity had to "be coupled with cultural continuity."[9] Simply put, African Christians had decided that embracing Christianity was fully compatible with and even required the affirmation of African culture and values. This was the exact opposite of missionary logic with its demand for converts to make a clean break with the pre-Christian spiritual-

ity of the continent. Fasholé-Luke's dictum, the principle of conversional continuity, has now become a bedrock conviction of almost all African Christians.
Even Catholics and conservative Protestant evangelicals, who initially resisted
the idea, now affirm the need to embrace rather than reject indigenous African
spiritual perspectives.

Christians in Asia reached a similar conclusion even earlier. In China, the
creation of a "three-self" (self-governing, self-supporting, and self-propagating)
church had been the goal of many Chinese converts and missionaries alike
since the late 1800s. When the Peoples' Republic of China was established in
1949, some Christians thought it might open the door to a truly independent
Chinese church. In 1950, forty well-known Protestant leaders in China drafted
a "Christian Manifesto" that emphasized both independence and anti-imperial-
ism. Their goal was simultaneously to create "a Chinese church whose affairs
are managed by the Chinese themselves" and to "make people in the churches
everywhere recognize clearly the evils that have been wrought in China by
imperialism; recognize the fact that in the past imperialism has made use of
Christianity; [and] purge imperialistic influences from within Christianity
itself."[10] In 1951, the Chinese Communist Party tried to co-opt this movement
by forming the state-sponsored Three Self Patriotic Movement and using it as a
pretext for persecuting uncooperative churches. The Communist intervention
was largely antithetical to the original three-self impulse, but some Chinese
Protestants went along, in part because the three-self principle was so deeply
engrained in Chinese Protestant thinking.

Meanwhile, Latin American Catholics were moving in the same general
direction, confronting the remaining vestiges of European power and question-
ing Western Christianity's anti-communist bias. Colonialism ended in Latin
America in the early 1800s, but the leaders of the Catholic Church had remained
largely European in their values and perspectives. In the mid-twentieth century, the Latin American Catholic Church still had a cozy relationship with the
region's conservative social elites and often paid little attention to the poor.
After the Communist takeover of Cuba in 1959, many Latin American oligarchs
turned to the military to protect their countries from a similar Communist
revolt and, by extension, to protect their own wealth. The entire region moved
toward the political right, and those who raised questions about social injustice
or economic inequality were declared to be subversives and were subjected to
harassment, arrest, or even execution. Many people simply disappeared.

In this repressive atmosphere, some Catholics began asking why the
Catholic Church seemed so comfortable with promoting law and order, which
had become code words for supporting the wealthy and disregarding the poor,
instead of seeking justice. A group of Catholics known as liberation theologians decided to address these matters directly by declaring that God actually

favors the poor and the oppressed. Liberation theologians criticized the region's right-wing military dictatorships, and they warned against letting outside powers (like the United States, which supported many of these right-wing dictators) tell Latin Americans as a whole or Latin American Christians in particular how they should structure their societies. The popular slogan of the time, "Yankee go home," was in many ways the Latin American equivalent of the African call for a moratorium on Western missionaries and the Chinese demand for a fully three-self church. It was an expression of independence and a refusal to any longer be told by outsiders what to think and how to act.

By the late 1970s, the overall global configuration of Christianity had become something very different than it was at the beginning of the century. A combination of faltering confidence in the Christian West (now frequently called the global Christian North) combined with growing self-confidence in the Christian South ushered in a new era of global Christian egalitarianism. Today, Christianity has no single center. Instead, it is a highly complex, multicentered, and hugely diverse global religious movement unlike anything the world has seen before.

Notes

1 "Requerimiento," https://kdhist.sitehost.iu.edu/H105-documents-web/week02/Requerimiento1513.html (accessed August 27, 2020).
2 Juan Ginés de Sepúlveda, quoted in Luis N. Rivera, *A Violent Evangelism: The Political and Religious Conquest of the Americas* (Louisville, KY: Westminster/John Knox, 1992), p. 220.
3 Antonio de Montesinos, quoted in Bartolome de Las Casas, *Witness: Writing of Bartolome de Las Casas*, translated by George Sanderlin (Maryknoll, NY: Orbis, 1993), p. 6.
4 Pope Benedict XVI, "Faith, Reason and the University Memories and Reflections," University of Regensburg (September 12, 2006), https://familyofsites.bishopsconference.org.uk/wp-content/uploads/sites/8/2019/07/BXVI-2006-Regensburg-address.pdf.
5 Edward Johnson, *Wonderworking Providence of Sion's Savior in New England* (1653), https://ia601805.us.archive.org/14/items/johnsonswonderw00john/johnsonswonderw00john.pdf (accessed August 27, 2020).
6 Rudyard Kipling, *Kipling: Everyman's Library Pocket Poets* (New York: Random House, 2007), pp. 96–98.
7 John R. Mott, *The Evangelization of the World in This Generation* (New York: Student Volunteer Movement for Foreign Missions, 1901), pp. 1–3.

8   Quoted in Richard Wright, *The Color Curtain: A Report on the Bandung Conference* (London: Dennis Dobson, 1956), p. 136.

9   Edward Fasholé-Luke, "The Quest for an African Christian Theology," *The Ecumenical Review* 27:3 (1975), p. 267.

10   Francis P. Jones, *The Church in Communist China: A Protestant Appraisal* (New York: Friendship, 1962), pp. 53–54.

7

The Contemporary Geography of Christianity

Christianity today is the largest and most evenly distributed religion in the world. In 1900, almost 70 percent of the world's Christians still lived in Europe, another 15 percent lived in North America, and only 15 percent lived in the Global South. Today, the distribution of Christians across continents is remarkably uniform: Africa, Europe, and Latin America each contain about 25 percent of the world's Christians, Asia is home to 15 percent, and the remainder (about 10 percent) live in North America. No other religion comes close to being so evenly spread around the globe: 99 percent of all Hindus reside in Asia (the vast majority in India), and so do 99 percent of all Buddhists (with about 80 percent located in the four East Asian nations of China, Japan, Thailand, and Myanmar). Islam, the world's second largest religion, is slightly more dispersed, but two-thirds of the world's Muslims continue to reside in Asia, and most of the other third are located in northern Africa (see Figure 7.1).

The global profile of Christianity has changed so much during the last century that it is tempting to describe Christianity as literally having been turned upside down. The previously dominant Global North (Europe and North America) is now, in terms of Christian numbers, only half the size of the Global South (Africa, Asia, and Latin America). But these numbers tell only part of the story. In addition, Christians in the Global South are energized; they see themselves as representing the Christianity of the future. The era when Europe dominated the Christian world is looking more and more like a mere parenthesis in the long story of Christianity. The deep history of Christianity is global, and after a relatively brief episode of Eurocentrism it has become global once again.

Mapping Christianity's Regional Differences

Using the two broad categories of Global North and Global South to describe the big picture of Christianity's changing demographics can be helpful, but these two regions do not by themselves convey any sense of how amazingly

What Is Christianity? First Edition. Douglas Jacobsen.
© 2022 John Wiley & Sons Ltd. Published 2022 by John Wiley & Sons Ltd.

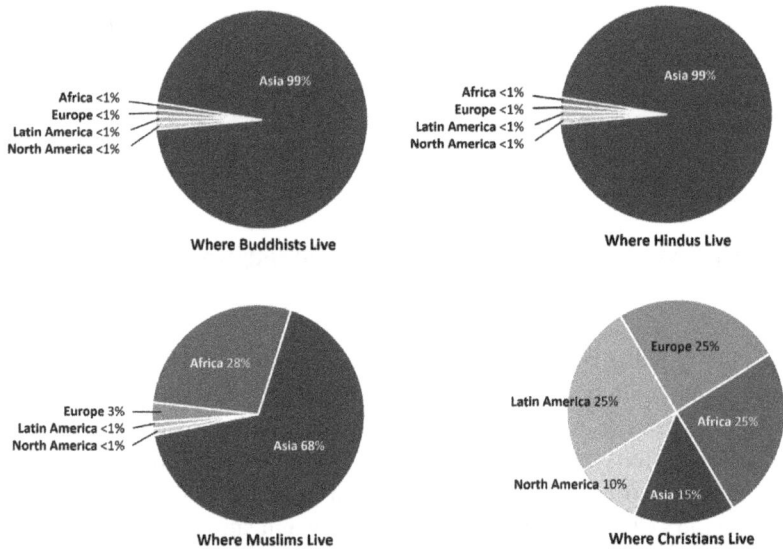

Figure 7.1 Global geographic profiles of the world's four largest religions.

diverse the global Christian movement has become. Christians in Africa, Asia, and Latin America are all categorized as living in the Global South, but they are not at all identical. Likewise, Christians in the United States and in Europe live in distinctly different religious worlds even though they are both considered to be part of the Global North.

Making sense of contemporary Christianity requires more nuance and detail than any bipolar vision of the world can convey. Every local context – or even every individual – brings a unique set of questions and affirmations to the practice of Christianity. In some regions of the world, Christians are persecuted, while in others they are not. In some locations, Christians are wealthy; elsewhere they are poor. In some places, Christianity has only recently been introduced; in other places, Christianity has been part of the landscape for centuries. Even more foundationally, the cultures of each region ensure that marriage and family relations are different, governmental philosophies vary considerably, and health care systems and social safety nets are either more or less existent. Every national and local society also has its own unique set of values, aesthetic preferences, and assumptions about what is public versus private.

Taking all of these factors into account, nine regions of the world can be identified as distinctly different environments where Christians are seeking to live out their faith today. Roughly in the order in which Christianity was introduced to each, these nine world regions are: (1) the Middle East and North Africa; (2) Eastern Europe; (3) Western Europe; (4) India and Central Asia; (5) sub-Saharan

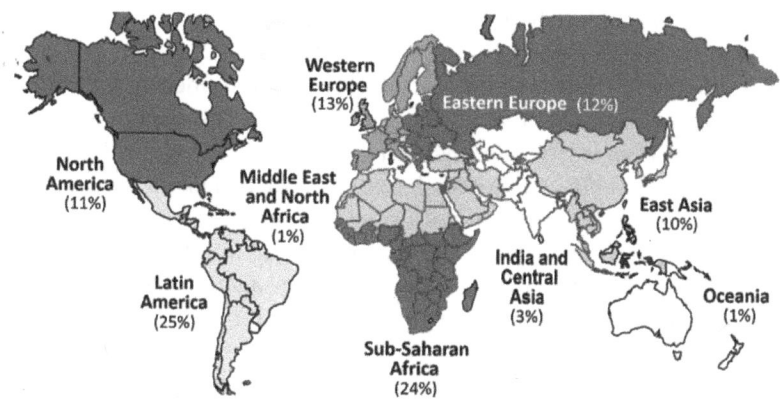

Figure 7.2 Nine regions of the world, with percentage (in parenthesis) of world's Christian population.

Africa; (6) East Asia; (7) Latin America; (8) North America; and (9) Oceania[1] (see Figure 7.2). Each of these nine regions shares a common history and each is also characterized by a constellation of values and norms that are shared by most of the people in the region. That said, no area is entirely uniform. The broad generalizations that apply to these territories as a whole do not describe everyone living in them. This nine-region map of the world provides at least a taste of the diversity of contexts in which Christians live today. Asking and answering the question "What is Christianity?" yields very different responses in each.

The Middle East and North Africa (1 percent of all Christians worldwide)

Christians in the Middle East and North Africa live on a razor's edge, always on guard, always wary that violence may erupt. In this region of the world, Christians are tolerated at best, and many Christians are exhausted by the unrelenting pressure of living in a place where the majority Muslim population views them as socially and religiously inferior. Some Christian families with the means to do so are leaving the region. A desire to escape was not always part of the local Christian mentality. Just thirty or forty years ago, Muslims and Christians often were congenial neighbors and friends, but the space for convivial interfaith relationships has shrunk as social and political tensions have increased. Most of the Christians who remain in the region are proud of their ethnic/national identities. They are confidently Palestinian, Persian, Syrian, Egyptian/Coptic or whatever, but simultaneously the slow grind of prejudice mixed with political instability is taking its toll, and Christians in this region of the world are becoming weary.

Interventions by Christians from outside the area, even when these Christians are well intentioned, have often made matters worse. This pattern of harmful consequences from interventions gone awry stretches all the way back to the Crusades of the twelfth and thirteenth centuries. Foreign interference has contributed to negative Muslim attitudes about Christians, and it is local Christians who have paid the price. The Iraq War, which began in 2003, further destabilized the region and encouraged Islamic radicalism, and Iraq subsequently lost about two-thirds of its Christian population due to the ravages of war and increased anti-Christian prejudice.

Another foreign involvement of continuing consequence is Western Christian support for Israel. Christian residents of the Middle East and North Africa almost uniformly view Israel as an unjust state. This is in part a reaction to Israel's treatment of Palestinians, but many Christians join their Muslim neighbors in thinking of Israel as the last remaining vestige of Europe's colonial presence in a land where it does not belong. The nation of Israel was created as the culmination of Jewish Zionism, but it would never have become an independent nation in 1948 without support from the West and especially from Great Britain and the United States. The trigger was the Holocaust and the need to establish a safe haven for Jews, but many Middle Easterners say that homeland should have been carved out of Europe, not here. Palestinian Christians are especially dismayed by the unquestioning patronage that Israel receives from so many foreign Christians and by the lack of support they feel from fellow Christians. The West's backing of Israel fuels anti-Christian sentiments in the region, and region, and it makes life harder for local Christians.

The demographic composition of Christianity in the Middle East and North Africa is unique. About half the region's Christians are Oriental Orthodox (Miaphysite), a third are Catholic, and one in ten is Eastern Orthodox. Only a relative handful of Protestants and Pentecostals live in the region. This was the heartland of the early Christian movement, but today Christians comprise only a small fraction of the general population. In 1900, about 10 percent of the population was Christian; today that number is down to 4 percent and is still declining.

Christians who remain in the region have two basic options: to be nice and try to keep a low profile and avoid trouble or to organize themselves and overtly defend their civil and religious rights. Neither option has been particularly effective. The self-effacement required by the first option (sometimes called the monastic option) reinforces the second-class status of Christians. The problem with the second option (sometimes called Christian nationalism) is that there are too few Christians to make it work. No matter how well organized they may be in any given nation, Christians don't have enough political clout to aggressively protect themselves. Accordingly, most Christians in the region are simply hanging on. They are tired and sometimes discouraged, but this region is their home and they are loath to leave it.

Eastern Europe (12 percent of all Christians worldwide)

After being severely restricted for decades under Communist rule during the twentieth century, Christianity has rebounded in the twenty-first century and has once again assumed a prominent role in the public life of Eastern Europe. Individual religiosity has also rebounded. In Russia, for example, only about a quarter of the population said they believed in God in 1990, but today at least 80 percent believe in God, with half expressing absolute certainty that God exists. Christian practices like going to church on Sunday have also rebounded, although they remain noticeably scarcer than in pre-Communist days. Eastern Europe's post-Communist revival of religion is unevenly distributed geographically. Relatively high levels of religious practice and devotion are evident in Poland, Romania, and Slovenia; measures of observable religiosity are lower in Estonia, Latvia, and Bulgaria. The majority of Christians in this region (about 70 percent) are Eastern Orthodox; roughly a quarter are Catholic, and more than half of those Catholics live in Poland. Only a few Protestants and Pentecostals reside in the region, but individuals from these groups are usually not shy about making their voices heard.

Over the decades of Communist rule, trust in government had slowly diminished to near zero. When Communism collapsed, many Eastern Europeans looked to the churches to help rebuild a sense of public trust and restore commitments to the common good. For a brief period of time the churches embraced this role, but more recently the energy of many churches has been directed away from social concerns and toward the maintenance of their own power and privileges. Many churches now see social liberalism as a greater threat to Christianity than antidemocratic authoritarianism.

In most of the Orthodox countries in the region, church leaders and national leaders now work closely together. This is blatantly obvious in Russia, home of half the region's population, where leaders of the Orthodox Church meet regularly with top government officials and carefully coordinate efforts to limit the religious rights of non-Orthodox Christians. In Romania, the Orthodox Church has invoked every possible legal and political mechanism to maintain possession of Catholic properties it confiscated during the years of Communist rule. And, in the Balkans, the post-Communist revival of religion resulted in an even more troubling outcome, a war of genocidal intensity between Serbian Orthodox Christians and their Catholic and Muslim neighbors.

The revival of Catholicism in post-Communist Eastern Europe has followed the same pattern as the Orthodox revival, with Poland serving as the prime example. The Catholic Church was a major player in Polish efforts to end Communist rule, partnering with Solidarity (the trade union that later became a political party) to unite the country. In the heady early days of freedom in the 1990s, Poles expressed overwhelming trust in the Catholic Church and its support for the common good. But times have changed, and the Catholic Church has shifted toward the political right, aligning itself with the conservative Law and Justice party. The Church today directs much of its energy to concerns about sexuality and gender identity and is a vocal advocate in favor of ever tighter restrictions on abortion and LGBTQ rights, even though Poland's current laws are already the most restrictive in Europe.

Whether they are Catholic or Orthodox, and wherever they are located, the churches of Eastern Europe are generally supportive of the various anti-immigrant nationalist movements that are now flourishing in the region. For a brief moment of time following the collapse of Communism, the churches of Eastern Europe were champions of freedom and democracy, but that sense of openness and optimism has faded. Instead of looking toward a better future, many of the Christian communities in Eastern Europe are now opting to anchor their identities in a romanticized vision of what they perceive to be their more glorious Christian past.

Western Europe (13 percent of all Christians worldwide)

Christians are still a majority in Western Europe, but their numbers have declined significantly during the last century. In 1900, roughly 95 percent of the Western European population was Christian. Today the percentage is down to 70 percent, and that includes a large segment of non-practicing Christians who never attend church, rarely think about Jesus, and hardly ever read the Bible or pray. Only about a quarter of the people living in this region believe in God as described in the Bible, and most say religion is a relatively unimportant part of their lives. Despite these statistics, many Western Europeans still think of themselves as Christians and embrace Christian *values*, which they largely equate with being good, caring people.

About two-thirds of Western Europe's Christians are Catholic, and the remainder are mostly Protestant. There are negligible numbers of Eastern Orthodox and Pentecostal Christians. On average, the decline in religious practices and beliefs is slightly more pronounced in predominantly Protestant countries than in predominantly Catholic nations, but the differences are small. For both Catholics and Protestants, the current decline in religiosity seems to have taken place for no specific reason at all. It was not the result of either persecution or oppression; Christians in Western Europe simply lost interest in their religion.

Today, the overall religious ethos of Western Europe is pervasively secular, but that fact alone does not convey the whole story. Some signs of Christian vitality do exist. For example, millions of people now engage in religious pilgrimages (many more than in the recent past), and millions of individuals also participate in organizations like Sant' Egidio (a Catholic NEM that serves the poor) or in programs like the Alpha Course (a multiweek seminar-style introduction to basic Christianity that was developed by evangelical Anglicans but that is also used by numerous Catholic churches in Europe). Perhaps the most vibrant expressions of Christianity in Western Europe are now found in the region's immigrant communities, where churches like the Nigerian-based Redeemed Christian Church of God are intentionally seeking to re-Christianize the continent. The recent influx of Muslims, often wearing traditional garb, has made religion much more visible in Western Europe, and it is unclear if this might spark a revival of Christian identity or simply solidify secular sentiments.

India and Central Asia (3 percent of all Christians worldwide)

The Christians who live in India and Central Asia are few in number, but they approach Christianity with an attitude of confidence. Indian Christians claim roots going all the way back to the first century when the Apostle Thomas arrived and introduced the gospel to the region. Based on their long local history, Indian Christians consider themselves to be every bit as authentically Indian as anyone else in the country, and they resent being described by some of their Hindu neighbors as insufficiently Indian, an attitude expressed with increasing intensity in recent years.

Modern India was created in 1947 as a predominantly Hindu but legally secular nation that showed no special favor toward any particular religion, but the current government, under the auspices of the BJP (Bharatiya Janata) political party, champions the public philosophy of *Hindutva*, asserting that India is and ought to be a distinctively Hindu state. Since 2000, supporters of *Hindutva* have intermittently terrorized India's non-Hindu people (both Christians and Muslims), often with the tacit approval of the government. More than half of India's Christians are Dalits (formerly called untouchables), and their low social status has made them particularly vulnerable to *Hindutva*-inspired violence.

In India and in Central Asia generally, Christians have historically clustered together in particular subregions, and this remains true today. Significant Christian populations are located in northern Kazakhstan (mostly Orthodox Christians); the Punjab province of Pakistan (half Catholics and half Protestants); Sri Lanka (mostly Catholics); the southernmost Indian states of Kerala and Tamil Nadu (a mix of different Christian groups that all trace their roots back to St. Thomas); and India's eastern states of Meghalaya, Mizoram, and Nagaland, where Protestants now constitute a majority of the general population. In the rest of the region, Christianity has only the thinnest presence. For the most part, Christians in India and Central Asia have been content with their status as religious minorities, and they have been committed to living peacefully alongside their neighbors of other faiths. In fact, some of India's most well-known Christian leaders have identified religious coexistence as a charism, a special spiritual gift, of Indian Christianity. This is not the uniform perspective of all Christians, however, and it is especially not true of Christians living in Nagaland in eastern India. In Nagaland, Baptists, who represent the majority of the population, have been waging a low-grade war against the Indian central government for decades, hoping eventually to gain independence and establish their own separate Baptist nation.

Sub-Saharan Africa (24 percent of all Christians worldwide)

Christianity in sub-Saharan Africa is growing faster than anywhere else on earth. Christianity is not new to the region: Ethiopia has been Christian since the fourth or fifth century, and Portuguese missionaries began introducing Catholicism along the continent's west coast in the late 1400s. However, the huge expansion of Christianity in the region did not begin until the twentieth century, and it accelerated in the 1960s and 1970s after the colonial era ended. Currently, more than half the region's population is Christian, and south of the Congo the percentage rises to 75 percent or more. Given current birth rates, more Christians will soon live in sub-Saharan Africa than any other region on earth. Those high birth rates also translate into sub-Saharan Africa having a younger population than any other region. The median age in Africa is now about nineteen, compared to thirty worldwide and to forty in the United States and Europe. Christianity in Africa is the religion of young people, which offers a stark contrast to the elderly ethos of many Christian communities in Europe and North America.

African Christian growth has enhanced the region's influence, and African Christianity has now become a powerful shaping force in Christianity around the globe. Much of this influence leans in a conservative direction, opposing what African Christians see as the moral laxity of the West. LGBTQ issues are especially prominent, and being supportive of LGBTQ rights is sometimes deemed heretical. The worldwide Anglican Communion split over this very issue, with Anglicans from Africa leading the way. In 2008, Africans helped to organize GAFCON (Global Anglican Future Conference) as a conservative organizational alternative to the international Lambeth network of Anglican churches which is overseen by the Archbishop of Canterbury. This division has continued even though the Archbishop of Canterbury (Justin Welby, elected in 2013) is a charismatic evangelical. Some African Catholic leaders, like Cardinal Robert Sarah from Guinea, have taken equally conservative positions within the Catholic Church, strongly favoring continued clerical celibacy, fervently opposing the ordination of women, and bemoaning the Western Catholic Church's leniency toward both divorced individuals and members of the LGBTQ community. A handful of African leaders have championed a more liberal and embracing message of Christianity, but progressive perspectives are clearly in the minority.

The true heart of African Christianity is not found in its conservativism, however, but in its belief in the spiritual vitality of the entire universe. In contrast to the disenchanted, mechanistic vision of reality that is so common in the modern educated West, most Africans believe that the universe is alive with spiritual energy and power. The visible material world and the invisible spiritual world overlap, interpenetrate, and interact with each other. African traditional religion acknowledges this dynamism, and many African Christians – including many conservative Catholics and evangelical Protestants along with Orthodox Christians and progressive Protestants – now argue that Christianity has to embrace and learn from this traditional African source of wisdom. This same attitude helps to explain the amazing growth of Pentecostalism in the region, which includes both a surge in explicitly Pentecostal churches and the absorption of many Pentecostal emphases by Africa's various non-Pentecostal churches. Pentecostalism, which is equally at home in the visible and invisible worlds, aligns with what Africans already believe and has the added appeal of providing protection from evil forces. Pentecostalism is flourishing all around the world, but it is uniquely at home in sub-Saharan Africa.

Any discussion of Christianity in sub-Saharan Africa must include the story of Ethiopia. The current size of its Christian population places Ethiopia among the top ten Christian countries in the world, but its history is what makes Ethiopia truly exceptional. The Ethiopian Orthodox Tewahedo Church, which is theologically Miaphysite, traces its Christian roots back to the fourth century but, according to Ethiopians themselves, the biblical roots of the country are much older. They believe that the Queen of Sheba (the ancient name for Ethiopia) visited Israel's King Solomon in the tenth century BCE, and the son born as a result of that encounter became King Menelik I. Ever since, Ethiopians have considered their kingdom to be partly Jewish. Even today the Ethiopian Orthodox Church celebrates a double sabbath (that includes both Saturday and Sunday), and every local church contains a *tabot*, a carved slab that symbolizes the tablets of the original Ten Commandments that were kept inside the ark of the covenant in the Jerusalem Temple. Ethiopia was Christianized in the mid-300s and was one of the first nations to adopt Christianity as its official state religion. The Ethiopian Christian Empire lasted until 1974, making it the longest-lasting Christian state in history. Ethiopia is now an officially secular nation and Christians make up less than two-thirds of the population, but Black Christians throughout the world continue to celebrate Ethiopia as a place where faith has been thoroughly Christian and proudly African for centuries.

East Asia (10 percent of all Christians worldwide)

The Christian population of East Asia is unevenly dispersed. Two-thirds of East Asia's Christians live in just two countries: the Philippines and China. Adding Indonesia and South Korea to the mix brings that number up to 90 percent. In most of the nations in the region, Christianity has only a small presence. Christianity is often located in ethnic minority communities, so Christians are frequently double minorities, experiencing both ethnic and religious prejudice at the hands of their neighbors. This is especially obvious in Laos, Myanmar, and Thailand where Christianity is almost entirely limited to the various hill tribe people that live in the northern regions of these countries while it is largely absent from the majority Lao, Burmese, and Thai populations.

Christian circumstances differ markedly from country to country. In China, Christianity's status has been volatile. Christians in China suffered during the early decades of Communist rule (in the 1950s, 1960s, and 1970s), then they were allowed increasing freedom during the years of openness to the West (the 1980s to the early 2000s), and oppression began to reoccur when Xi Jinping came to power in 2013. In South Korea, the situation is dramatically different. Christians make up about 30 percent of the population, and they have considerable political power, as evidenced by the fact that half the nation's presidents have been Christians. In the Philippines yet another dynamic is apparent. Christians make up the vast majority of the population and most are Catholic, but a decidedly anti-Catholic politician (Rodrigo Duterte) was elected president by the Filipino people in 2016 despite explicit opposition from the Catholic Church. This is part of a larger rift that has emerged between Catholic Church leaders and the Filipino laity, who seem intent on making their own moral and political choices independent of any instruction from their bishops and priests. Indonesia presents still another scenario, where religion is divided along the lines of geography. The eastern part of the country is largely Christian, the west is overwhelmingly Muslim, and in the middle region, where the two groups overlap, violence has sometimes occurred.

Many East Asians view religion differently than it is viewed in the West. Rather than assuming that individuals will associate with only one religion at a time, East Asians generally think it is perfectly acceptable to embrace a number of different religions simultaneously. Religions are viewed as complementary rather than contradictory or competitive. Each religion offers people a distinctive package of spiritual insight and assistance that is more or less helpful in different life situations. For example, a decision about who to marry raises very different spiritual questions than how best to reverence the dead or what job to pursue. An East Asian individual might consult Taoism for help with the first question, Confucianism for assistance with the second, and Christianity for guidance about the third. This understanding of religion makes the Western notion of *belonging* to a single religion seem a bit nonsensical. Religions don't own people; instead, people use or participate in different religions as needed. Historically, this kind of fluid and flexible religious pluralism has been rejected by most Christians worldwide, but it has always been part of the Christian mix in East Asia, and it is currently becoming more common elsewhere.

Latin America (25 percent of all Christians worldwide)

A quarter of the world's Christians now live in Latin America, where both Catholicism and Pentecostalism are flourishing. (Protestants and Orthodox Christians have only small toeholds in the region.) This is a significant change from the situation that existed in the mid-twentieth century. At that time, Catholicism had a near monopoly over religion in the region, and the Catholic Church had grown somewhat lethargic. With no other viable options to consider, many Latin Americans were Catholics by default. Then, over the course of the past half century, Catholicism lost its monopoly, and its percentage of the population dropped from roughly 90 percent to under 70 percent. However, Catholicism's loss in numbers unexpectedly sparked a spiritual revival within the Catholic Church itself. The option to not be Catholic made being Catholic a conscious choice, and the act of choosing led to stronger faith commitments. As a result, Latin America has become the new heartland of global Catholicism, and its churches are perceived as models for the rest of the Catholic world.

The current spiritual vitality of Latin America is not solely a Catholic phenomenon; it is intertwined with the ascent of Pentecostalism. Pentecostalism first appeared in the region in the early twentieth century, but it exploded across the region in the 1970s, 1980s, and 1990s, and it continues to thrive today. One out of every five Christians in the region is now Pentecostal. Initially, Catholic leaders were incensed that Pentecostals were "stealing their sheep," converting Catholics away from Catholicism and thereby putting Catholic souls at risk. Some Catholic bishops and priests actively denounced Pentecostalism, and some still do. In Mexico, for example, Catholic families sometimes are encouraged to put signs on their doors telling *evangélicos* (a term used to describe both Protestants and Pentecostals) to stay away. But censuring Pentecostalism did not stop it from growing, and a number of Catholic leaders decided to fight spiritual fire with spiritual fire by pouring their support into the Catholic Charismatic Renewal (CCR), which offered Catholic believers a Spirit-filled Catholic alternative to *evangélico* Pentecostalism. Today, there are more members of the CCR than there are members of all the Pentecostal denominations combined, and in most places Catholic–Pentecostal relations have improved. The ending of Catholicism's religious monopoly and the rise of religious pluralism have resulted in a stronger and healthier Catholic Church and a more robust practice of Christianity in general.

Latin America's new spiritual vitality is not only charismatic and church-revitalizing, it is also committed to social justice. Latin America has been plagued by social and economic inequality ever since the colonial conquest in the 1500s, and Latin American Catholics have always known that their Church was complicit in justifying and maintaining those inequalities. In the 1960s and 1970s, civic liberty and social equity emerged as goals championed by a group of Catholic leaders known as liberation theologians. Liberation theology asserted that God has a preferential love for the poor and dispossessed, and it called the Catholic Church to repentance for its past practices. Over time, the Catholic Church did largely repent, and the moral terrain of the whole region shifted as a result. Today, concern for justice permeates not only the Catholic Church, but many other churches in the region. Christians in Latin America assume that faith and the economy cannot neatly be separated into two domains; no one can love God while turning a blind eye to the needs of the poor.

North America (11 percent of all Christians worldwide)

Of the nine global regions, North America is the most visibly Protestant. The United States has been predominantly Protestant since its earliest days, and even in Canada, which was first colonized by French Catholics, Protestants have been the majority of the population for most of the nation's history. The region is less Protestant today than ever before, but an ethos of Protestantism remains, and this is especially evident in the emphasis put on religious freedom. Religious freedom has played an enormous role in the social histories of both Canada and the United States. Most North Americans agree with the Protestant assumption that faith is authentic only when it is freely chosen by the individual with no strings attached. In many regions of the world religious identity is assigned at birth, but in North America the consistent emphasis has been on the right to practice (or not to practice) the religion of one's own choosing.

As much as they may value their own religious freedom, North Americans have sometimes been complicit in denying religious liberty to others. Up until the twentieth century, for example, Catholics in the United States were often treated with disdain because their faith seemed incompatible with the nation's commitment to personal religious freedom. In reaction to this pattern of social bias, American Catholics constructed their own separate "parochial" (as opposed to "public") school system to protect their children from Protestant influence and Protestant prejudice. Even more egregiously, white North American Christians restricted the human rights as well as the religious rights of Black slaves. Enslaved persons often had to worship in secret if they were going to worship God at all, and when they were sometimes allowed to join in the worship services of the region's white-run denominations they were typically sequestered in some corner of the room or forced to stand at the back of the sanctuary. In response, Black American Christians created the African Methodist Episcopal (AME) Church in 1816 as the first explicitly anti-racist denomination in North America. Even after the Civil War and the ending of slavery, the nation's white-controlled churches continued to treat Black Christians with disdain, and a variety of other predominantly Black denominations were formed in response, incuding the National Baptist Church (1880) and the Church of God in Christ (1897). The Civil Rights Movement of the 1950s and 1960s helped to diminish overt racism in the region, but most churches remained divided by race. Even today, more than fifty years later, Sunday morning remains the most racially segregated hour of the week.

As a percentage of the population, Christianity has been slowly declining in North America for decades, but an especially steep drop took place in the early 2000s and the Protestant majority was especially hard hit. In 1900, roughly 80 percent of the region's population was Protestant; today it is only about a third. Even if Pentecostals are added to the Protestant column, which is a common practice of researchers and journalists, the expanded total barely reaches 50 percent. The growth of Catholicism, which increased from 15 percent of the population in 1900 to just over 20 percent today, explains some of Protestantism's decline, but the far more significant factor has been the increasing number of North Americans who describe themselves as nonreligious. These individuals are not necessarily atheistic or attitudinally antireligious, but they are thoroughly dis-enamored with *organized* religion and have no interest in affiliating with any church or other religious organization. Nonreligiosity is much more prevalent among younger people (ages eighteen to thirty) than it is among older adults, which may signal a difficult future for organized, church-based Christianity in the region.

At present, evangelical Christians are the largest and most visible religious subgroup in the region. Once an entirely Protestant movement, American evangelicalism has expanded in recent decades to include many Pentecostals and even some Catholics. The defining religious characteristic of evangelicalism is being "born-again," experiencing a spiritual rebirth that initiates a lifelong personal relationship with Jesus Christ. Over the last half century, however, a different feature of the movement has slowly become more prominent. While being born-again still matters, evangelicalism is now very closely associated with right-wing politics and, in the United States, with the Republican party. More than 80 percent of American evangelicals voted for Donald Trump in 2016 and nearly as many voted for him again in 2020, even though Trump's personal lifestyle is thoroughly out of sync with evangelicalism's espoused moral values. Many evangelicals fear that North American culture is becoming anti-Christian, and they are relying on their Republican political allies to defend their religious rights and to protect them from possible persecution. It is precisely this evangelical alliance with the political right, however, that is driving many Americans away from evangelicalism and away from Christianity in general.

Oceania (1 percent of all Christians worldwide)

Two very different plots are unfolding in the story of Christianity in Oceania, and what separates these subplots is race. The storyline of the indigenous people of the Pacific (including indigenous Australians, Torres Strait Islanders, Maoris from New Zealand, and Pacific Islanders) centers on their massive recent conversion to Christianity. Missionary activity in the region did not begin in earnest until the nineteenth century, but today about 90 percent of the indigenous population is Christian. In Oceania, conversion has typically meant an explicit rejection of older ways of life and an enthusiastic embrace of Christianity, but this dynamic is becoming less predictable. Some indigenous Australians, for example, are seeking to recover their old ways of life and merge them into their still steadfast Christian identities. Anthropologists have sometimes denounced Christianity for destroying Pacific cultures and spirituality, and there is some truth to these accusations. Most indigenous Christians in the region have a different view, however. For them, Christianity has been an unambiguously positive step forward both for themselves and for their cultures.

The second plotline of Christianity in Oceania concerns the European settler population, and it is a narrative about decline. White people began arriving in the region in the late 1700s, and the first settlers were prison convicts who had been exiled to Australia from Great Britain. Despite significant resistance to *wowzerism* (overly zealous faith), Christianity gradually took hold within the immigrant European population, and by the time the united Commonwealth of Australia was created in 1901 around 95 percent of the white population was Christian. Today, however, only half the white population is affiliated with a Christian church. Nowhere else in the world, not even in Europe, are Christian numbers declining more rapidly, and nowhere else, even in North America, is the regional story of Christianity more obviously bifurcated along the lines of race.

Christian Interactions Today

The main storyline for Christian history over the last fifty to a hundred years concerns the global growth and stunning diversification of the movement. Countless variations and modifications have been added to the Christian movement, and an unprecedented level of contact and awareness now exists among different kinds of Christians worldwide. Many contemporary Christians are keenly aware that their own particular expression of Christianity represents only one of many ways that people can be Christian. Christians worldwide now swim together in a sea of Christian differences, and it is harder than ever before to make the case that that one's own particular Christian church or sub-tradition is unequivocally the best or most complete version available.

Christianity has been globally diverse throughout its history, but very few Christians in previous centuries experienced that diversity in their everyday lives. This is no longer the case. Different varieties of Christianity no longer exist only in distant lands; different kinds of Christians now reside side by side with each other on the same street. Seventy-five years ago, most Christians still lived in places where almost all the other Christians they met looked and acted just like them. In 1950, roughly 80 percent of all Catholics lived in countries and neighbourhoods that were almost entirely Catholic. That same dynamic of religious homogeneity likely held true for 95 percent of Orthodox Christians and at least half the world's Protestants. In recent years, that kind of religious homogeneity has noticeably declined. Today, only about half of all Catholics live in predominantly Catholic locales (mostly in southern Europe and Latin America), and only 10 to 20 percent of Protestants remain in predominantly Protestant territory. A large majority of Orthodox Christians continue to reside in areas that are mostly Orthodox, as they have for centuries, but new Pentecostal churches are popping up almost everywhere in the world, even in the Orthodox heartlands.

Christian practices from all the traditions and from all geographic regions are now being juxtaposed in new and more intimate ways as Christian immigrants move from country to country around the globe. Today, roughly 75 million Christians live in a country that is not where they were born. Some of these Christians are refugees who have been forced to flee their homelands, some are temporary international workers, and some have moved elsewhere because of marriage or simply to build a new life for themselves and their families. Together, they constitute only about 3 percent of the world's total Christian population, but they are having an immense impact on global Christianity. In most European and North American cities, it is relatively easy to meet and interact with – or some might say it is hard to avoid meeting and interacting with – Christians from Africa, Asia, and Latin America. In New York, there are now almost 200 African immigrant Christian congregations spread across the city, and every week Catholic mass is celebrated in more than forty different languages in Los Angeles. Christians from Africa, Asia, Europe, Latin America, and North America are on the move around the world, and in most of the world's larger cities, as well as in many smaller cities, Christianity is currently represented in a multitude of cultural and linguistic forms.

Proximity inevitably leads to more social interactions, and those routine contacts have allowed Christians around the world to discover similarities and differences with other groups of Christians that they had never heard of before. As a result, some Christians have become more willing to look beyond the norms of their own group and to try to benefit from the cumulative wisdom and insights of newly arrived groups. Other Christians who have been exposed to Christianity's contemporary diversity have, however, reacted differently, clustering together more closely in order to protect themselves from new ideas and to reinforce the beliefs they already hold dear. Regardless of their responses, there is no going back to a time when a particular church or tradition could naively assume that their kind of Christianity represented the entire movement. Christians around the globe now recognize that Christianity comes in many different shapes and flavors.

When Christianity came into existence two thousand years ago, it quickly developed into a diverse movement that attracted people from many different regions and cultures. Rather than dividing along ethnic lines, however, these early Christians kept talking to each other, and sometimes arguing with each other, about what it meant to be a faithful follower of Jesus. Something similar seems to be happening today. Christians from around the globe and from all

Christian traditions are discovering each other and engaging in new conversations, sometimes congenial and sometimes intense, about what it means to be a follower of Jesus in the contemporary world.

Note

1 For more information on these nine regions see Douglas Jacobsen, *The World's Christians: Who They Are, Where They Are, and How They Got There*, 2nd edition (Chichester, UK: Wiley/Blackwell, 2021).

8

Common Threads and Shared Challenges

Christianity as it exists around the world today is so diverse that some observers now write about Christianities (in the plural) rather than Christianity (in the singular). They have a point. Christianity today is not only incredibly varied, it is also riven with conflicts that sometimes appear irreconcilable. And yet, differences and disputes do not tell the entire story. From the beginning of the movement until today, Christians have shared much in common.

It is important to remember that Christianity began as a movement and that it remains a movement today, a reality that limits what should be expected in the way of commonalities. Movements are loosely structured human associations, tenuously held together by a range of mutual goals and motives that are more-or-less compatible but not always fully consistent. People join movements for different reasons, and sometimes reasons change. Movements are maintained by interpersonal relationships and bonds of affective commitment, and a movement can fade when friendships falter or commitments fade. Christianity has seen its fair share of splintering over the centuries, but Christianity retained its identity as a single movement even as it divided into a wide variety of separate and distinct churches. It is this broad but interconnected character of Christianity that provides the focus here, rather than one particular churchly tradition or one specific region of the world. This chapter begins by looking at the shared ideas and values of Christianity before its first major splintering in the Great Divide of the sixth century and then turns attention to the common orientations and challenges that define the global Christian movement today.

Common Threads in the Early Christian Movement

Gathering information about common beliefs and practices within early Christianity is complicated by the fact that that early Christianity was largely an underground movement. Its members had to be very cautious about what they said and how they said it because Christianity was a minority religion that lacked legal standing. The movement was also socially suspect; some people looked at Christianity askance because they believed Christians were cannibals. The symbolic language of eating the body and blood of Christ that was used to describe the bread and wine of the Eucharist was taken literally, and they concluded that Christians actually ate human bodies and drank human blood in their closed-door meetings for worship.

So Christians had to be careful, and prudence led them to develop code languages to help them identify each other, a semi-secret collection of symbols and phrases likely to be understood by other Christians but not by the general public. One well-preserved example of this coded speech comes from a tomb inscription of an individual named Abercius (or Avirvius) who died in western Turkey around the year 200. It begins by noting that Abercius traveled widely throughout the ancient world, so its references probably would have been meaningful to Christians from all those places. It reads in part:

> I am the disciple of a holy shepherd who feeds flocks on mountains and plains, who has powerful eyes keeping everything in view. For he it was who taught me...Everywhere I had kindred spirits. Faith led the way everywhere and set before me as nourishment everywhere a fish from a spring, immense, spotless, which a holy virgin caught. And this she gave into the hands of her friends to eat always, having good wine, giving mixed wine with bread...May the one who understands and is in harmony with all these things pray [for me].[1]

The inscription describes specific elements that would enable other Christians to recognize the deceased as one of their own. It alludes to a holy shepherd (which is how Jesus was often depicted in early Christian art), to a fish (the letters of the Greek word for fish were used by Christians as an acronym for the phrase "Jesus Christ, Son of God"), to a holy virgin, to wine and bread mixed together (which is how the Eucharist is still distributed in today's Eastern Orthodox churches), and to the efficacy of prayers for the dead. If these references identified Abercius as a kindred spirit to other Christians, then it seems safe to assume they were commonly embraced by many Christians in the second century. These items – the kindly humanity and simultaneous divinity of Christ, Mary's special role in salvation history, celebration of the Eucharist, and praying for the dead – are surely not a complete description of Christianity, but their inclusion indicates their likely prominence.

As the Christian movement began to coalesce into more organized local communities of believers, various clusters of Christians began to develop their own lists of what Christians held in common. These statements were intentionally brief so that converts were required to affirm only a handful of central beliefs before being welcomed into fellowship. One of the earliest examples is a document called the Roman Symbol, which was used by the church in the city of Rome during the third century. It is composed of three questions which the Bishop of Rome would ask candidates for baptism and church membership before welcoming them into fellowship:

> Do you believe in God the Father All Governing? Do you believe in Christ Jesus, the Son of God, Who was begotten by the Holy Spirit from the Virgin Mary, Who was crucified under Pontius Pilate, and died and was buried and rose the third day living from the dead, and ascended into the heavens, and sat down on the right hand of the Father, and will come to judge the living and the dead? Do you believe in the Holy Spirit, in the holy Church, and in the resurrection of the body?[2]

The Roman Symbol is far more focused on beliefs than the Abercius inscription, and there is little overlapping content between the two. The only explicitly shared point of reference is a holy virgin. However, it should be kept in mind that these statements were written for very different purposes. The Roman Symbol was an institutional statement about Christianity, trying to clearly articulate some key elements of Christianity's emerging system of beliefs; it was not, like the Abercius inscription, a coded document meant to be understandable to Christians but baffling to outsiders. The shortness of the Roman Symbol, both what it includes and just as importantly what it does not, indicates that it was not designed as a quiz to keep people out of the church. Quite the contrary, the Symbol was meant to include rather than to exclude, and it gained rapid popularity within the movement precisely because of this *catholic* (inclusive) quality. By the fifth century it was being widely used throughout the Christian world, and eventually the Symbol was reworked and expanded to create the so-called Apostles' Creed, which is still used as a statement of faith in many churches today.

As the Christian movement expanded into new territories and became more culturally diverse, it became increasingly difficult to identify beliefs and practices that all Christians shared in common. In the fifth century, the French monk Vincent of Lérins (d. 445) recognized this problem and decided to provide a solution. He would empirically examine the entirety of Christian history and then write a book describing the handful of Christian convictions that had never changed. These beliefs and practices, marked by their "universality, antiquity, [and] consent," could then provide a standard for Christians everywhere.[3]

Vincent quickly realized that his goal was impossible. He found very little that all Christians had affirmed in common throughout all of Christian history, so he shifted his focus to what "almost all priests and doctors" of the church had always believed.[4] This adjustment allowed Vincent to complete his task, but it also put a thumb on the scale. Set free to selectively accept or reject differing historical views, Vincent ascertained that what *almost all* Christians had believed in the past was very similar to what he himself believed and, not coincidentally, to what the Roman Imperial Church believed. His final compilation of common Christian convictions looked very much like the conclusions of the Council of Ephesus which had been held just a few years earlier, in 431. Rather than producing an empirical description of Christianity, Vincent wrote a book that offered selective historical support for what he and his church had already agreed all Christians ought to believe.

After the Council of Chalcedon (in 451) and the Great Division that followed in its wake, the search for common threads of Christian belief and identity was largely abandoned. For well over a thousand years, almost all the world's Christians were content to view Christianity only and solely through the lens of their own particular Christian church or community. From their own perspectives, their way was the right way and every other Christian pathway was wrong. Little, if anything, was open for discussion. The idea that Christianity *as a movement* was bigger, more diverse, and more inclusive than any single organized, institutionalized churchly expression of Christianity became almost incomprehensible, and for hundreds of years this constricted thinking dominated the Christian movement.

The Modern Search for Christian Unity

About a century ago, there was a revival of interest in the notion of Christianity as a broad movement that transcends its various ecclesiastical embodiments. Christian missionaries were among the first to move in this direction. They focused on the basic elements of Christianity when they tried to explain Christianity to new converts abroad, and it gradually dawned on them that Christians of many different stripes really do share much in common. Unexpectedly, awareness of Christianity's diverse expressions around the world also made it easier to discern common threads. The cluster of traits that most Christians share in common seemed much more obvious in global perspective than it did close up, in the same way that shared family traits are often more apparent at large gatherings of an extended family than they are in smaller and more limited family settings.

This revival of interest in Christianity's commonalities eventually gave rise to the Ecumenical movement of the twentieth century. The noun "ecumenism" and the adjective "ecumenical" are derived from a Greek term that means "one house," and ecumenical Christians of different theological and ecclesiastical persuasions see themselves as part of one big household or family of faith. Christianity's new ecumenical impulses eventually led to the creation of the World Council of Churches (WCC) in 1948. The WCC focuses explicitly on the visible unity of the Christian churches, and it seeks to moderate or reverse ecclesiastical fragmentation by emphasizing cooperation among churches and by mutually affirming shared convictions. At present, the WCC has about 350 member churches, and all of them are committed to reducing their religious animosities and highlighting what they share in common.

Not all Christians with ecumenical inclinations have become involved in the formal Ecumenical Movement, however. Many have instead sought to encourage Christian unity through more informal and less institutional means. A prime examplar of this is the British author C.S. Lewis (1898–1963), whose book *Mere Christianity* has become a modern ecumenical classic. Lewis's book picks up Vincent of Lérins's original challenge and tries to identify certain beliefs and practices as "common to nearly all Christians at all times,"[5] and Lewis vowed to be rigorously empirical. He said his own theological preferences were of no consequence; his book would include only those items that Christianity had always proclaimed, whether or not he liked them. To check his own prejudices, Lewis asked clergymen from four different Christian churches (Anglican, Catholic, Methodist, and Presbyterian) to read his manuscript and point out any biases. According to Lewis, they found none.

Lewis described Christianity's commonalities using the adjective *mere*. He was looking for the basics, the minimal framework of belief that people had to possess in order to consider themselves Christian. He viewed 'mere' Christianity as something like the skeleton of a body or like the foundation of a building. It is not the entirety of Christianity, but it is essential. Lewis's most common metaphor was that of a boarding house with a long common hallway and many separate guest rooms. Mere Christianity, he said, was like the common hallway. It represents what all Christians hold in common and through which they must walk in order to arrive at their own guestrooms (the churches to which they belong). Lewis made it clear that mere Christianity is not Christianity itself. It does not come close to capturing the fullness of faith that is embodied in the lives of Christians. What mere Christianity represents instead is the shared core of values and convictions that allows Anglicans, Catholics, Methodists, Presbyterians, and members of many other churches to collectively call themselves Christians. It is their common affirmation, the glue that binds together the broad Christian movement.

Lewis's description of mere Christianity is not a list of doctrines. His description reads much more like a worldview, a narrative of faith that captures the essence of the Christian message. In Lewis's merely Christian vision of reality, God exists, Jesus is the Son of God, and Jesus makes salvation possible. However, Lewis also places a great deal of emphasis on ethics. In particular, he argues that morality is not a matter of opinion; good and evil are objectively written into human nature and into the universe as a whole. Furthermore, Christianity is rational. Being a Christian is not the only reasonable pathway of life that people can choose, but faith in Christ is an eminently reasonable way of life, not a leap into the dark.

Mere Christianity moved far beyond the narrow woodenness of many creedal affirmations and infused ecumenical discussions of Christian commonalities with a new level of energy and logic. Lewis provided a winsome interpretation of Christianity, but like every book ever written it reflects its own place and time. In particular, *Mere Christianity* was written in Great Britain when that nation still ruled a vast region of the world through its colonial empire. Lewis had imbibed the self-confidence that characterized British imperial Christianity as a whole, and his status as an Oxford professor made him even more certain of his own ability to assess Christianity fairly and accurately. While he asked clergymen from four different churches to provide feedback, all of them were his former students (who were likely prone to agree with his views) and their churches clearly do not represent the full spectrum of Christianity. It likely never dawned on Lewis to solicit feedback from Christians living outside of Europe, and it is possible that he had never heard of Pentecostalism. Moreover, *Mere Christianity* was written at a time when traditional gender roles were still often construed as moral imperatives. Lewis enthusiastically embraced that perspective, a viewpoint that many (but certainly not all) Christians today would find jarring or even antithetical to the gospel. The cultural residues that adhere to *Mere Christianity* do not negate the book's importance, but they certainly limit its usefulness as a timeless and universal description of Christianity's essential core.

A generation after Lewis wrote *Mere Christianity*, Pope John Paul II offered an alternative and more nuanced perspective on the common threads that exist within Christianity. In contrast to the stay-at-home Lewis, who rarely ventured outside of Great Britain, Pope John Paul II was the most widely traveled pope in history. He visited more than 125 nations during his years in office (1979–2005), and he was thoroughly aware of the vast cultural differences that exist across Christian communities around the world. Trying to make sense of all that he had seen and heard, the Pope developed a new appreciation for both the unity and the diversity of Christianity. His book *Crossing the Threshold of Hope* describes the Christian movement as a work still in progress. Instead of looking for common threads solely in the beliefs and practices of the past (which was the tack taken by both Vincent of Lérins and C.S. Lewis), Pope John Paul II understood Christianity's complex unity-in-diversity to be something that was still evolving. Deeper and richer insights might continue to emerge from increasing exposure to the "plurality of ways of thinking and acting [and] of cultures and civilizations"[6] within the Christian movement. In other words, Christianity's common threads of faith are not only woven into the Christian past; those commonalities are still in the process of being formulated and reformulated in the present.

Christian Commonalities Today

Crafting a description of what Christians hold in common remains a difficult task today, but that task has been made easier both by increased awareness of other religions and by secularism. Thus, for example, the Christian practice of treating Sunday as a holy day may not have been perceived as anything distinctive when most Christians lived in places where a seven-day week, starting with Sunday, was a simple fact of life. Knowing that other religions structure the calendar differently, however, and now living in a time when many non-religious activities are scheduled on Sundays in the same way they would be scheduled on any other day, makes a seven-day week that begins with Sunday stand out as uniquely Christian.

The Christian movement today is far too varied for anyone to develop a list of beliefs and practices that are embraced literally by all Christians everywhere. (Some Christians might want to tell all Christians what they *ought* to embrace, but that is not the same thing.) The approach taken here is impressionistic, focusing on those things that are generally-held-in-common by most (but certainly not all) Christians. This looser style of defining Christianity applies to many other subjects, as well. For example, it is very difficult to make a comprehensive list of all the elements an activity must possess in order to be considered a game. Most games involve competition, but some games do not; neither the game of solitaire nor the game of hide and seek require competition. Similarly, most games have a definite end point, but others (like the game of tag) do not and can go on forever until the participants decide to stop. Nevertheless, most people can still explain what makes a game different from merely engaging in play. In the same way, there is almost nothing that absolutely all Christians share in common, but it is still possible to describe Christianity in general. In the following description, three categories of commonalities are highlighted: practices of worship, doctrines and beliefs, and the spiritual grammar that underlies Christianity's view of ethics and salvation.

Common Worship Practices

The vast majority of Christians around the world gather for worship on Sundays (though some meet on Saturday), and most Christians, if they can afford it, meet for worship in a building (a church, cathedral, or temple) that is specially designated for that purpose. Catholic and Orthodox Christians tend to think of these buildings as distinctively sacred places for meeting God; Protestants and Pentecostals are much less likely to see the building itself as sacred, but most Protestant and Pentecostal churches still include a "sanctuary," a room that is set aside for worship. When they gather for worship, most Christians sing songs of praise to God, they engage in corporate prayers that request God's assistance for themselves and others, and they celebrate the Eucharist (sometimes called Communion or the Lord's Supper) which points toward Christ's death in the past, toward fellowship among Christians in the present, and toward future, metaphorical banqueting in heaven. Christians have a wide array of views about how Christ himself is present in the Eucharist, ranging from the Catholic notion of transubstantiation (that the bread and wine of the Eucharist become the actual body and blood of Jesus), to a view commonly held by Protestants that Christ's presence is purely symbolic. Catholics, in particular, encourage Christians to celebrate the Eucharist frequently, even daily if possible; Communion is offered much less frequently in most Protestant and Pentecostal churches. With the exception of a small handful of Protestant groups, baptism is considered to be necessary for church membership, and most Christians also see baptism as necessary for salvation, though some Protestants and Pentecostals might disagree.

Throughout their history, most Christians have followed a yearly Christian calendar that sets some days apart for fasting and prayer and designates other days as times of holy celebration. Catholics, Orthodox Christians, and many of the older Protestant churches (Anglican, Lutheran, Reformed) place great importance on this church calendar and organize their worship schedules around it; some Protestants and many Pentecostals largely ignore it. Almost all Christians, however, celebrate at least two Christian holy days (holidays) in common: Christmas, focusing on the birth of Christ, and Easter (also called Pascha), focusing on Christ's resurrection from the dead. For many Christians, Easter is preceded by forty days of fasting and penance called Lent. Easter is an unusual holy day because its date varies from year to year based on the Jewish lunar calendar. Eastern Orthodox Christians determine this date using a different calculation than Catholics, Protestants, and Pentecostals, which means that all Christians celebrate Easter on the same day only once every three or four years. Many Christian churches use a lectionary, a schedule of selected readings, to guide their reading of the Bible in public worship. The Catholic Church and many Protestant churches follow a shared three-year cycle of lectionary passages that cover almost the entire Bible. Orthodox churches follow a shorter schedule that repeats every year. Many Pentecostal and evangelical Protestant churches do not follow any set schedule for Bible reading. Their selection of scriptural readings to be included in worship is determined either by the minister's sermon topic or by the needs and inspiration of the moment.

Common Christian Doctrines

All Christians consider Jesus to be a special religious teacher whose message they seek to follow. Almost all Christians also consider Jesus to be God incarnate, and the standard description of Christ's nature is that he was simultaneously both fully human and fully divine. Not all Christians believe in God – some people link their Christian identity to Christian values without any reference to God – but the vast majority of Christians believe in God as the Creator and Sustainer of the world, and almost all of them believe that God is best described as a Trinity comprised of Father, Son, and Holy Spirit. Christians have never agreed on one best way to explain the three persons of the Trinity and how they relate to each other and the created order, but affirmation of God as a Trinity is a key belief that distinguishes Christianity from the other two Abrahamic religions of Judaism and Islam. It took centuries for Christians to develop the formal doctrine of the Trinity, but the idea that God is somehow three-in-one has been prevalent almost from the beginning, and it remains ubiquitous today. Some Unitarians, people with a Christian background who deny the doctrine of the Trinity, still call themselves Christians, but many do not. Christianity's core beliefs are primarily based on the Bible, which all Christians view as a sacred text and many believe to be inerrant or infallible. The precise meaning of the Bible has always been open to debate, however, and this is one reason why Christianity is so internally diverse. Even when two Christians agree that the Bible is inerrant, there is no guarantee that they will reach the same interpretive conclusions.

Common Spiritual Grammar

Christians around the world share a handful of basic assumptions about humanity's relationship with God and about the responsibilities that people owe to each other; these assumptions function like the rules of grammar in a language. Christianity's spiritual grammar is built on the premise that the world as it currently exists is not the world as it was meant to be. This not-rightness of people and of the world in general is called sin or fallenness, and Christians believe that God is in the process of undoing the world's defectiveness and making all things right. This setting aright of human lives and of the world as a whole is called salvation. To those who have been harmed by sin (almost everyone, but some more than others), God offers healing, liberation, and justice. To those who have committed sins (everyone), God offers reconciliation through a process of confession (the recognition of one's own contribution to the brokenness of the world), repentance (the willingness to change one's ways and attempt to set right the things one has helped to make wrong), and divine forgiveness.

Christians generally believe that God must initiate the process of salvation (this divine initiative is called "grace") and that human beings can never fully heal or reform themselves or the world on their own. Almost all Christians believe that Christ's death and resurrection were somehow required in order for salvation to occur, but various Christian groups explain this differently. Christians also believe that God has commanded them to love everyone in the same way that they love themselves, and this is part of making the world right. Numerous other religions affirm this same rule of love, but that does not make it less essential. Not all Christians live by the rule of love, but it is the ultimate standard by which Christians judge themselves and their actions in the world.

Contemporary Challenges

Looking at Christianity *from the inside* out provides one perspective for ascertaining the common contours and characteristics of Christianity; looking at Christianity *from the outside* in provides another. As a religion, Christianity is known not only by its common commitments but also by its relationships with and differences from other faiths and ways of life, and Christianity is currently confronting four major challenges at these boundaries where Christianity and otherness meet. One of them is an old issue that has assumed new prominence in recent years: Christianity's connections with various local indigenous religions. A second challenge centers on Christian–Muslim relations. The third challenge concerns the recent upsurge in non-religiousness (or religious disaffiliation) around the globe. Finally, Christianity is confronting the more nebulous but daunting spiritual challenge of learning to live in the Anthropocene era, a new epoch in world history when humans have themselves become the dominant force shaping the planet's environment.

Christianity and Local Religions

As late as 1900, about a quarter of the world's people still practiced local religions. These religions had no names; they were simply the embodied ways of life that local people had followed for as long as they could remember. Scholars now refer to them with labels like African traditional religion, Chinese folk religion, indigenous religion, or primal religion, but none of the participants in these traditional ways of life would have used such terms. The idea of "religion" itself, understood as something separable from life in its totality, would have been incomprehensible. In local, traditional contexts, religion is part of the seamless fabric of life. It is not something that anyone has to think about or decide to engage. It is not one aspect of life versus any other. It is simply the way the community functions and, from the local perspective, it is how the world has always worked.

During the last century, many of these localized, traditional ways of life have been seriously weakened or have disappeared entirely as people who formerly followed indigenous ways of life have converted to one or another "world religion." The phrase "world religion" is itself a modern invention that was developed in the mid-twentieth century. World religions were those that appeared to transcend the bounds of local idiosyncrasy and that offered more comprehensive, philosophical ways of explaining their views and practices to followers. These world religions were also geographically expansive, including members from numerous different cultures and nations. Indigenous religions were considered, by contrast, to be idiosyncratic and localistic, with little potential to expand beyond their immediate environs. This was clearly not a values-free description of either kind of religion, but it was widely embraced.

The four largest contemporary world religions are Christianity, Islam, Hinduism, and Buddhism, but lists often include other systematized and well-organized religions like Jainism, Judaism, Sikhism, and Zoroastrianism. Conversion to one or another of these world religions has sometimes been voluntary, but not infrequently indigenous people have been encouraged or even forced to convert. In Indonesia, for example, all local religions were banned in the late 1960s and every person was required to join one of the government's six approved world religions: Buddhism, Catholicism, Confucianism, Hinduism, Islam, and Protestantism. (Indonesia treats Catholicism and Protestantism as two different religions, not as two varieities of the same religion.) In the early twentieth century, roughly half of all Indonesians followed local religious traditions; today that number is less than 1 percent.

Many local, indigenous religions have largely disappeared from sight, but they have certainly not disappeared from people's lives. Pockets of traditional life exist around the world, and some indigenous leaders are trying to preserve and restore what remains. This is especially evident in Latin America, where numerous indigenous rights movements have evolved since the 1990s, and similar developments can be observed in Australia, Southeast Asia, and North America. Many traditional religions have also maintained their influence through a different mechanism: by functionally uploading some of their key elements into the world religions that have sought to replace them.

This merging of world religions and local religions is possible because the claims and practices of most indigenous religions do not compete head-to-head with the beliefs and practices of most world religions. Most local religions focus on practical wisdom. They help people negotiate their way through the world as it is. By contrast, most world religions have a salvational dimension. They describe the world and human beings as defective in some way and then provide a way of salvation that delivers change and improvement. In almost all world religions, however, there is some lag time between the promise of salvation in the present and the fullness of salvation as people hope to experience it in the future. In that interval between the already and the not-yet, there is a niche where local religions can offer their practical wisdom to people who are negotiating the complexities and moral difficulties of life in the here and now. Not every local practice and perspective will be preserved, but some of them will survive the winnowing and will remain in use, safely embedded in a world religion.

Christianity has a long history of mixing and merging with local religions. Medieval encounters in Western Europe involved a host of different tribal traditions and pagan ways of life. In the sixteenth and seventeenth centuries, Latin America was awash in encounters with indigenous religions. Some observers argue that Christianity's engagement with the capitalistic civil religion of North America represents a similar phenomenon: Christianity trying to grapple with an alternative, not inherently Christian but not necessarily anti-Christian set of religion-like values, desires, and moral principles.

Historically, the religious mixing and merging of Christianity and indigenous faith has proceeded haphazardly with little attempt to systematically evaluate the results, but in recent years this has changed, and many Christians are now actively exploring connections. Africa is the current hot spot for Christian-indigenous interaction. Many Western Christians still worry about the possible reframing of classic theological tenets, but nearly all the African churches have come to believe that as much as possible of local, traditional religious wisdom should be preserved within Christianity. How much inclusion is possible requires discernment, and Africa's endeavors are encouraging Christians in many other locations to think anew about how their lived practices of faith should (or should not) be shaped by local religious customs and values.

Christianity and Islam

Christianity and Islam share many characteristics. Both are monotheistic religions, both venerate Jesus (Muslims even affirm the virgin birth of Jesus), and both look toward a time when God's intentions for the world will finally be perfectly fulfilled on earth. Christians stress God's forgiving character and Muslims stress God's mercy, but these attitudes are more or less equivalent. The major difference between the two religions concerns the Prophet Muhammad. Muslims believe the message of the Quran delivered through the Prophet supersedes the message of Christ, and Christians reject that assertion. (It should be noted, however, that many Christians make the same claim about their own faith's relationship to Judaism: that Christianity transcends or replaces Judaism.)

Muslim–Christian relations have never been easy. During the first hundred years of Islam's existence, Muslim armies captured huge swaths of previously Christian-controlled land, and almost none of that territory has ever been regained by Christians. Church buildings were sometimes transformed into mosques, and some Christian practices like the ringing of church bells or public processions were prohibited. Military-political-religious tensions have divided Muslims and Christians ever since. The historic low point of relations came in the twelfth and thirteenth centuries when Western Crusader armies attacked Muslims in the Middle East, followed by an equally troubling Islamic backlash against Christianity in Persia and Central Asia in the fourteenth and fifteenth centuries. Things settled down after that, and in some regions of the world Christians and Muslims lived side by side in relative peace. Occasionally, Muslims and Christians even became cordial neighbors and friends who celebrated each other's holidays together.

This live-and-let-live ethos has declined precipitously during the last hundred years. In the early 1900s, the Ottoman Empire was still the main social carrier of Islam, but it was disbanded following World War I and large swaths of the Islamic world were colonized by the Christian West. Many Muslims felt like they were being subjected to a new kind of crusade as they were once again invaded by Christian military-political occupiers. Muslim leaders in many countries developed deeply anticolonial attitudes, and in some cases that anticolonialism morphed into generalized disdain for the West and its religion of Christianity. This attitude eventually gave rise to Islamic fundamentalism, represented by groups like Al-Qaeda, Boko Haram, Hamas, Hezbollah, ISIS, al-Shabaab, and the Taliban. These are fringe groups within Islam as a whole, not the mainstream, but taken together they form a substantial fringe, and Christian perceptions of Islam have shifted as a result.

Islam's stunning growth has also exacerbated tensions with Christianity. At the beginning of the twentieth century, about 12 percent of the global population was Muslim, putting it roughly on par with Buddhism and Hinduism. Today, Islam claims a quarter of the world's people, which means that Muslims now outnumber Buddhists by a factor of three to one and that Islam is almost twice as large as Hinduism. In 1900, Islam was one religion among several prominent alternatives to Christianity; today it is unequivocally Christianity's main religious competitor, and the competition for souls has intensified. In recent decades, Muslim–Christian conflicts have flared throughout the Middle East, in Central Asia, in the Balkans, in East and West

Africa, in Western Europe (which has become a popular destination for Muslim immigrants), and in Southeast Asia. For some contemporary Christians and for some Muslims, being *against* the other group has become a major component of their religious identity.

The rising level of hostility between Christians and Muslims has made the world a much more dangerous place. Together, Christians and Muslims comprise more than half the population of the planet. If the world is to survive, followers of these two religions need to develop better perceptions of each other and healthier working relations. Whether this is possible is unclear. Both Christianity and Islam are presently divided into internally opposed camps – one favoring reconciliation and the other hankering for battle – and it is uncertain which of these tendencies will prevail in either faith.

Christianity and the Religiously Unaffiliated

A hundred years ago, only a handful of mostly European intellectuals identified as either secular or non-religious. Today, about 15 percent of the world's population is religiously unaffiliated. Some of these individuals are convinced atheists and a few are actively anti-religious, but many are simply disenamored with or distrustful of religion. They may still believe in God and may even consider themselves to be spiritual in some sense, but they do not feel any need to align themselves with an organized religious association like a church, mosque, or synagogue. Religious disaffiliation is unevenly distributed around the globe. It is most common in Europe and it is rarest in Africa, but it is a growing phenomenon everywhere. Nonreligion is also divided along generational lines, with younger people being much more likely to say they are religiously unaffiliated than older people.

It is not yet clear whether this kind of nonreligion or secularity is a passing phase in human history or a permanent change, but it is deeply troubling to many Christians. The underlying issue is not new. As early as the 1940s some Christian leaders, like the German theologian and anti-Nazi activist Dietrich Bonhoeffer, had already noticed a shift away from traditional religion to post-religion and had expressed concern about the implications for Christianity. Some other Christians were less alarmed about religion's declining popularity because they claimed that Christianity wasn't really a religion at all. Karl Barth was perhaps the most famous Christian theologian to make this claim, saying that religion was humanity's effort to reach upward to God, while Christianity was the result of God reaching downward in Jesus to save humankind.

Barth's distinction is clear but not necessarily fully accurate. Rather than being an either/or choice between Jesus and organized religion, Christianity seems to be much more of a both/and phenomenon. Many Christians do consider their personal relationship with God to be the core of their faith, not their church affiliation, but it is difficult to see how Christianity could have survived over the centuries apart from the institutional framework provided by Christianity as an organized religion. Spirituality deriving solely from a personal relationship with the divine is hard to maintain. Human affections are skittish, and handing down a purely personal faith from generation to generation is almost impossible. If Christianity had not been effectively institutionalized as a religion, it is likely that the memory of Jesus would have evaporated from earth long ago. Christianity endured because the inner experiences of Jesus's followers were externalized into the beliefs, practices, and institutional structures of an organized religion. This externalization of faith had a cost. Organized religions can make mistakes, and those mistakes are often publicly and painfully visible, but Christianity survived because it existed in the public sphere in addition to being a personal faith.

A comprehensive understanding of Christianity will take both the inner, personal side of faith *and* the externalized, organized, institutional side of faith into account. Right now, the external side of Christianity is garnering a significant amount of criticism, and perhaps it should. Organized Christianity has made a lot of very public mistakes in recent centuries, and Christians themselves are fully aware of this fact. That some people are leaving the ranks of organized Christianity in response is not surprising. What are the implications for the future? It is highly unlikely that Christianity will disappear anytime soon. While some evidence points toward greater secularity in the coming years, other data suggest that organized religion is likely to increase its share of the world population during the next half century. At present, many Christians feel that the institutional side of Christianity should be at least partly reined in so that individuals have more flexibility and freedom to pursue their own personal spiritual quests. To the degree that churches are able to accommodate this impulse, the growth of nonreligiousness may become, instead of a threat, an opportunity that stimulates followers of Jesus to deepen their faith in God and to heal some of their broken relationships with others.

Christianity and the Anthropocene Era

The fourth and final challenge facing Christians, along with all of humanity, is the rise of the Anthropocene, a new era in the biogeologic history of the planet. Its defining characteristic is that humans are now a key factor in determining the present and future livability of the world. Scientists are still debating when the Anthropocene era began, but it is common to date its origins to the years immediately following World War II when the fallout from the world's first nuclear explosions left an indelible imprint on the earth's surface and when the world's demand for land, food, energy, medicines, weapons, electronics, and almost everything else began to accelerate at unprecedented speed. There is no longer a place on earth that is totally natural or wild. Human beings have left their mark everywhere, and the future of the planet is now inextricably linked to human activity.

The Anthropocene era represents a challenge to Christianity because it calls into question one of Christianity's most enduring convictions: that ultimately God controls the world. During times of pain or struggle, many Christians reassure each other that as depressing as the present may seem, God is in charge and everything will ultimately be shown to have had a purpose. This sense of divine oversight has both personal and historical implications. For individuals, belief in God's sovereignty has often been a source of hope and endurance. Applied to history more broadly, the doctrines of divine omniscience and omnipotence have been a font of confidence in the future. If humans now largely determine the future, then this sense of Christian hope and confidence becomes much harder to maintain.

In the past, most Christians have adopted one of two interpretations of earth's future. Some Christians have assumed that God's influence in the world will gradually increase and that the "kingdom of God" eventually will dawn in its fullness. Other Christians have assumed the opposite, that the world will become worse over time until God dramatically intervenes to set things right. The Anthropocene adds at least two other possibilities: that human beings will end history in a nuclear conflagration or that their continued abuse of the natural world will slowly make the planet uninhabitable. Neither option invokes God at all, and neither prompts optimism. What does Christianity have to say to a world whose fate seems to be controlled by humans? An added complication is that the historically Christian nations of the world have been intimately involved in creating the Anthropocene Era and therefore Christians have in some sense created this problem for themselves.

Contemporary Christian attitudes vary tremendously. Some Christians argue that Christianity must become more ecologically supportive of the flourishing of the earth in its entirety and less singularly focused on humans and their salvation. Other Christians believe it is evil to place any limits on human productivity or population growth, regardless of the added stress it places on the planet. The challenges posed by the Anthropocene do not have simple or easy solutions. Nor do the challenges imposed by local religions or Islam or nonreligiousness. Instead, these four contemporary challenges underscore the need for Christians to continually reconsider their practices and beliefs as the world changes around them. This is not something new. Christianity has been changing and developing from the moment it was born, and the arguments and decisions of today are simply the next chapter in that long and dynamic history.

Notes

1 William Tabbernee, ed., *Early Christianity in Contexts: An Exploration Across Cultures and Continents* (Grand Rapids, MI: Baker Academic: 2014), pp. 5–6.

2 John H. Leith, ed., *Creeds of the Churches: A Reader in Christian Doctrine from the Bible to the Present* (Richmond, VA: John Knox Press, 1973), p. 23.

3 Vincent of Lérins, *Commonitorium*, 2:6, *New Advent*, https://www.newadvent.org/fathers/3506.htm (accessed July 31, 2020).

4 Vincent of Lérins, *Commonitorium*, 2:6.

5 C. S. Lewis, *Mere Christianity* (New York: Macmillan, 1952), p. ii.

6 Pope John Paul II, *Crossing the Threshold of Faith* (New York: Knopf, 1995), p. 153.

Conclusion

What Is Christianity Today?

Christianity is today what it has always been: a living religion in the process of formation and re-formation. It has been under construction since the time when Jesus first began preaching in ancient Galilee 2000 years ago. Jesus never wrote a guidebook for the movement, and he told his followers not to worry about planning but instead to trust God. He implored people to repent and get ready to participate in the kingdom of God that was already breaking into history, but he never described that kingdom in detail. Instead, he used parables and aphorisms to communicate his message and to orient his followers in a general spiritual direction. Those followers later came to believe that, after Jesus ascended to heaven, the Holy Spirit was sent to guide and empower the Christian community as it sought to build that kingdom on earth. As they continued that work, Christians have refined and sometimes redefined the goals and identity of their movement, and those efforts are still ongoing today.

At present, efforts to refine and define Christian faith are being carried out mainly within the confines of Christianity's four largest traditions – Orthodoxy, Catholicism, Protestantism, and Pentecostalism – and each of these traditions is being pulled and stretched in new directions by Christianity's recent re-globalization. This is not a new dynamic, however, since Christianity and its various traditions have been growing and changing for centuries, and traditions are never written in stone. Every tradition has a history, and every tradition also has a future that is being created by decisions in the present. The contemporary moment in Christian history is unique only because so many Christians from so many different nations and local cultures are simultaneously involved in the process.

This book has described Christianity empirically, tracing its historical developments through the twists and turns that have made it the religion it is today. This is a very different approach than the one taken by Adolph von Harnack when he delivered his famous lectures at the University of Berlin more than a hundred years ago. Harnack's goal was to identify the unchanging and unchangeable essence of Christianity, to define for all time what Christianity *was supposed to be*. This volume does not try to identify Christianity's essence, because the real

What Is Christianity? First Edition. Douglas Jacobsen.
© 2022 John Wiley & Sons Ltd. Published 2022 by John Wiley & Sons Ltd.

meaning of Christianity is not found in abstract spiritual ideals. Christianity is an incarnational faith, a living faith embodied in the lives of individuals and located in changing worlds of human understanding, action, and interaction. Consequently, this book describes how different groups of Christians have expressed their faith in varied and changing historic contexts and how Christian faith is being embodied in cultures and traditions around the world today.

Harnack himself was an historian, but his lectures were an attempt to abstract Christianity from history. He described Christianity as a timeless ideal that floated above the grit of human lives and the blemishes of church history. If this was merely Harnack's view, it could be dismissed easily as the musings of a bygone age, but many Christians, especially those who live in the Global North, continue to describe Christianity using theological and philosophical language that disconnects faith from history and from the flesh and blood lives of people around the globe.

In recent years, many Christians have become suspicious of definitions of Christianity that are ahistorical or overly idealistic, and they are giving greater attention to the concrete practices of Christians in different times and places. This approach is especially prominent in the writing of non-European Christians, and one of the most articulate spokespersons for this new style of Christian reflection is the Ghanaian theologian Mercy Amba Oduyoye (b. 1934). Oduyoye has taught at Harvard, lectured at universities around the world, and held key leadership roles in the World Council of Churches. She understands how Christianity operates at the educational and ecclesiastical summit of the movement where idealism often flourishes, but she also knows Christianity at the grassroots level where people have sometimes been harmed or oppressed by people claiming to act in Christ's name. As an African Christian, in particular, she says it is impossible for her to ignore the gap between "Christianity preached" and "Christianity lived." She writes that African Christians must deal every day "with racism among children of One God and... with the exploitation and dehumanization of the sister and brother for whom Christ died."[1] Oduyoye is a convinced Christian who longs to see Harnack's emphases on human interdependence and respect for all persons better embodied in contemporary Christian practices, but she never averts her eyes from Christianity's actual history where those ideals have often been ignored or undermined.

In her theological writings, Oduyoye gives special attention to the faith practices of African Christian women. Acknowledging that Christianity has often "reinforce[d] the depersonalization of women,"[2] Oduyoye founded the Circle of Concerned African Women Theologians in 1989 so that African women would have a place to talk about their lives and their faith in a space where men could not silence them or dominate the conversation. She insisted on the organizational structure of a circle, a framework for egalitarian conversation where no one has the power to control or censure the subjects and viewpoints under discussion. Any woman can participate, regardless of religious identity, as long as her goal is to think deeply about life and to be in dialogue with others.

The image of a circle can also be helpful as a way to understand the dynamics of global Christianity as a whole. Global Christianity now operates like a grand circle of conversation where people from many different Christian communities have the ability to engage others in open-ended dialog about what Christianity is and ought to be. From Oduyoye's perspective this is a positive development that allows the Christian movement as a whole to look at itself more realistically than it has in the past. Still, she worries that "predigested theologies" might be invoked to provide answers before questions are even asked and to cut off dialogue before it begins. Oduyoye insists that a living faith must ask where God is active in the world today and then wait to hear what people have to say, and it must listen carefully even when responses do not point in the same direction. Her conclusion is that Christianity is not and never has been a one-size-fits-all religion. The goal instead is for individuals and communities of Christians to be inspired by the efforts of others and then creatively to address the specific challenges and opportunities that exist in their own local contexts. Oduyoye explains: "There is no justification for demanding one uniform system of theology throughout the Christian community." The aim is to foster theologies that contribute in dfifferent ways to "the building up of a more righteous world."[3]

Christianity today is what it has always been: a complex movement of people trying to discern what it means to be followers of Jesus in a diverse and constantly shifting world. Christians have often sought to coordinate their visions of what they believe and how they are called to live, and this impulse toward consensus is alive and well today. But Christian history has also been shaped by reformers, prophets, heretics, and saints who have refused to follow majority opinions and who have launched out on their own, hoping to discover or invent better ways of understanding and incarnating the aspirations that Jesus proclaimed. Christianity has flourished because of this dynamic, a tale of balancing innovation with historical awareness and of balancing affirmation with communal critique. If there is a single essence to Christianity perhaps it is this: trying to follow the way of Jesus in a given time and place without knowing in advance what that might require. Emancipated from the burden of uniformity and timelessness, Christianity is the never-ending quest of followers of Jesus to be faithful to God and lovers of their neighbors in a world that never stops changing and developing.

Notes

1 Mercy Amba Oduyoye, *Hearing and Knowing: Theological Reflections on Christianity in Africa* (Maryknoll, NY: Orbis, 1986), p. 9.

2 Mercy Amba Oduyoye, *Daughters of Anowa: African Women and Patriarchy* (Maryknoll, NY: Orbis, 1995), p. 9.

3 Oduyoye, *Hearing and Knowing*, p. vii, 7.

Index

What Is Christianity? First Edition. Douglas Jacobsen.
© 2022 John Wiley & Sons Ltd. Published 2022 by John Wiley & Sons Ltd.